Robert Louis Stevenson

Author Study Activities for Key Stage 2/Scottish P6–7

Nikki Gamble

David Fulton Publishers

David Fulton Publishers Ltd
The Chiswick Centre, 414 Chiswick High Road, London W4 5TF

www.fultonpublishers.co.uk

First published in Great Britain in 2004 by David Fulton Publishers

Copyright © Nikki Gamble 2004

British Library Cataloguing in Publication Data
A catalogue record for this book is available from the British Library.

ISBN 1-84312-077-1

The materials in this publication may be photocopied only for use in the purchasing organisation. Otherwise, all rights are reserved. No part of this publication may be reproduced, stored in a retrieval system or transmitted, in any form, or by any means, electronic, mechanical, photocopying, recording or otherwise, without the prior permission of the publishers.

Author Study Series
Series editors: Eve Bearne and Helen Bromley

Also available in this series:

David McKee: Author Study Activities for Key Stage 1
by Sally Elding (ISBN 1-85346-934-3)

E. Nesbit: Author Study Activities for Key Stage 2
by Helen Bromley (ISBN 1-85346-933-5)

Michael Morpurgo: Author Study Activities for Key Stage 2
by Sally Wilkinson (ISBN 1-85346-927-0)

Cover design and poster design by Martin Cater
Designed and typeset by Kenneth Burnley, Wirral, Cheshire

Contents

Introduction v
Acknowledgements vi
Map of contents vii

1 Biographical information 1
   - Biographical activities 5
   - Extract notes 12
   - Photocopiable sheets 1.1–1.8 15–22

2 Robert Louis Stevenson: Classic author 23
   - Activity: Investigating classics 25
   - Photocopiable sheet 2.1 26

3 *Treasure Island*: Historical context 27
   - Treasure Island activities: Context 31
   - Photocopiable sheet 3.1 33
   - Activity: Book display – antecedents and sequels 34

4 *Treasure Island*: Narrative structure and plot 35
   - Activity: Design a theme park ride 38
   - Photocopiable sheet 4.1 40
   - Activity: Mood and suspense 41
   - Activity: Story openings 43
   - Photocopiable sheets 4.2–4.5 44–47

5 *Treasure Island*: Narration and point of view 48
   - Activity: Whose point of view? 50

6 *Treasure Island*: Characters 52
   - Activity: Long John Silver – hero or villain? 57
   - Activity: Character development and change 59
   - Activity: Character through dialogue 60
   - Photocopiable sheets 6.1–6.3 61–63

7 *Treasure Island*: Setting   64
- Activity: Designing a film set   66
- Activity: Sound collage   68
- Photocopiable sheet 7.1   69

8 *Treasure Island*: Themes   70
- Activity: The quest   72
- Photocopiable sheet 8.1   73

9 Adaptations   74
- Activity: Character and film   75
- Photocopiable sheet 9.1   76
- Activity: Investigating opening sequences   77

10 Three-week plan   78

11 Reading other books by Stevenson   85

12 Poster challenges   88

Select bibliography of Stevenson's works   90
Resource list and bibliography   91

Introduction

This author study guide is designed to be used flexibly so that you can either follow an in-depth study of Robert Louis Stevenson and his books (see three-week plan) or can select those aspects that relate to other literacy work you are planning. For example, you might choose to include Stevenson's travel writing in a unit on autobiography. Prior to starting this unit of work, you might choose to set up a stimulus display, and an extensive resource list is included (pp. 91–94) to facilitate the collection of supporting material. A lot of internet material has been produced about the author; if using the internet for research, children will need to consider how they can make judgements about the reliability of the information, taking the authorship of the material into account.

Acknowledgements

I would like to thank the students and teachers at the University of Cambridge, Faculty of Education and the University of London, Institute of Education who have helped with trialing these materials, and for their constructive feedback.

A special thank you to Alec, who had lots of interesting things to say about *Treasure Island*, and who fired me with enthusiasm.

Map of contents

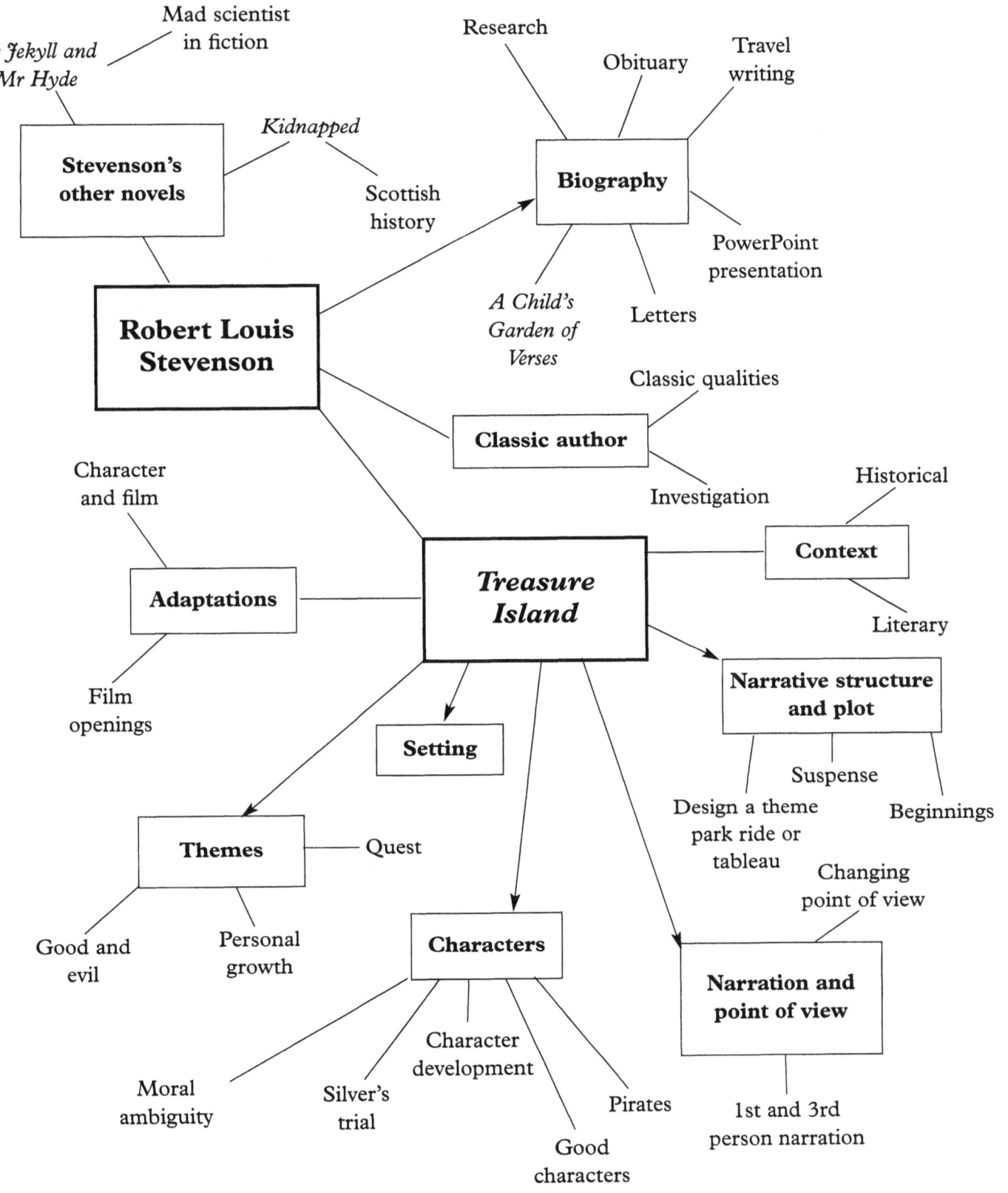

1 Biographical information

Robert Louis Stevenson (1850–94), classic novelist, poet, travel writer and essayist, is acknowledged as having had a significant influence on the development of children's literature. His body of work covers the major genres of writing of the nineteenth century (adventure, historical, horror, travel, poetry). His novels, *Treasure Island*, *Kidnapped* and *Dr Jekyll and Mr Hyde* continue to be read by young readers in various forms and have inspired many film adaptations, including *Muppet Treasure Island* and, most recently, Walt Disney's *Treasure Planet*. His collection of poetry, *A Child's Garden of Verses*, first published in 1885, is as fresh and appealing today and has never been out of print. Morag Styles pays tribute to his contribution to the genre in her history of children's poetry, *From the Garden to the Street* (1998): 'Robert Louis Stevenson is the single poet who gets a Chapter to himself in this book, despite writing only one volume of verse for children. The reason for privileging Stevenson in this way is the belief that *A Child's Garden of Verses* is 'a pivotal collection which changed for ever how children could be written for and about in poetry' (p. 170).

Early years

Stevenson was born in 1850 at Howard Place on the outskirts of Edinburgh's fashionable New Town. Baptised Robert Lewis Balfour, he was the son of Margaret Balfour, a minister's daughter, and Thomas Stevenson, a celebrated civil engineer. Stevenson's highly respectable parents were deeply religious and were devoted to their son, but their possessiveness was stifling and it is perhaps not surprising that Stevenson rebelled in his youth against the conventions of Edinburgh middle-class society.

Throughout childhood Stevenson suffered, as did his mother, from poor health, which persisted throughout his life until his untimely death at the age of 44. When he was 18 months old, the Stevensons employed a nurse, Alison Cunningham, to take care of their son. Cummie, as she was called, was immortalised in Stevenson's letters and in his dedication for *A Child's Garden of Verses*:

To Alison Cunningham

From her Boy

For the long nights you lay awake
And watched for my unworthy sake:
For your most comfortable hand
That led me through the uneven land:

> For all the story-books you read:
> For all the pains you comforted:
> For all you pitied, all you bore,
> In sad and happy days of yore: –
> My second Mother, my first Wife,
> The angel of my infant life –
> From the sick child, now well and old,
> Take, nurse, the little book you hold!
>   *A Child's Garden of Verses* (1885)

Stevenson later recalled how Cummie told him sensational stories from Cassell's *Illustrated Papers*, which fuelled his nightmares and probably influenced his taste for the grotesque. Although Stevenson did not learn to read until he was seven years old, he was recognisably precocious. His favourite childhood occupation was playing with Skelt toy theatres, which involved cutting out, decorating and assembling cardboard and paste sheets of scenes and characters. When finished, the theatre was used for re-enacting and inventing stories, literally bringing the magic of the theatre into the home. Later, in an essay in which he recalled the pleasure and formative experience of theatre play, Stevenson wrote: 'What is the world, what is the man and life but what my Skelt has made them?' He also enjoyed listening to stories, and particularly enjoyed adventures such as R. M. Ballantyne's *Coral Island* and James Fenimore Cooper's *The Last of the Mohicans*. The influence of these writers can be seen in the adventurous content of his own novels. Reflecting on his childhood, Stevenson wrote: 'I have three powerful impressions of childhood: my suffering when I was sick, my delights in convalescence at my grandfather's manse of Colinton, near Edinburgh and the unnatural activity of my mind after I was in bed at night.' These childhood memories are recalled in many of the poems in *A Child's Garden of Verses*, such as 'The Land of Counterpane' and 'Bed in Summer'.

Education and career

Stevenson was educated at Edinburgh Academy, and at 17 years of age became a student at Edinburgh University, where he followed the family tradition by studying engineering.

Stevenson's father was a prominent civil engineer who designed lighthouses and lighting apparatus, and his grandfather had built the Inch Cape lighthouse at the mouth of the Firth of Forth. Stevenson, however, did not want to be an engineer, so his father urged him to follow a legal career instead. Nevertheless, in 1875 after passing his law exams, Stevenson chose not to practise as a barrister. Instead he turned to writing, which had interested him since childhood. This choice of career caused problems with his father who referred to 'the devious and barren paths of literature'. Stevenson later wrote: 'All through my boyhood and youth, I was known and pointed out for the pattern of an idler and yet I was always busy on my private end which was to learn to write . . . indeed I had already my own private determination to be an author . . . I loved the art of words!'

The traveller

Stevenson enjoyed travel. 'For my part, I travel not to go anywhere but to go. I travel for travel's sake', he wrote. In particular, he had a passion for all things French, and changed his middle name from Lewis to its French form Louis, although he retained the Scottish pronunciation. In 1876, Stevenson set out with his friend Walter Simpson on a canoe trip down the River Oise through France and Belgium. He wrote about the expedition in his first book, *An Inland Voyage* (1878). In the book he expresses pleasure at having been suspected of being a Prussian spy by the French gendarmes, and pride at having endured hunger, cold and misery. A second travel book, *Travels with a Donkey* (1879), famously recounts a 12-day walking tour through France's Massif Central. Laden with a home-made sleeping bag, two changes of clothes, a spirit lamp, cooking pan, lantern, candles, jack knife, exercise book, some provisions and his companion, a donkey called Modestine, Stevenson set out to experience subsistence living. 'Night', he wrote, 'is a dead monotonous period under a roof; but in the open world it passes lightly, with its stars and dews and perfumes, and the hours are marked by changes in the face of nature.'

Family man

In 1877, during his European travels, Stevenson met and fell in love with an American, Fanny Osborne. Fanny was already married, ten years Stevenson's senior and had two sons. When she returned to America, Stevenson feared that he would not see her again. At the end of July 1879, against the advice of his friends, he set sail for America with the intention of persuading Fanny to marry him. He regarded the journey as a romantic adventure: 'Travel is of two kinds; and this voyage of mine across the ocean combined both . . . I was not only travelling out of my country in latitude and longitude, but out of myself.' The voyage was uncomfortable and his health suffered severely. When he eventually arrived in New York harbour after the arduous journey, he was compelled to wait days with the crowds of emigrants for the train to take him west to California. By now Stevenson was critically ill and in California he was close to death. But the journey was ultimately a success: Fanny was divorced in December 1879 and married Stevenson in San Francisco on 19 May 1880. In August, Stevenson and his bride returned to Scotland and were welcomed to his parents' home in Heriot Row.

Writing

Stevenson continued to suffer from poor health in the years 1880–87, but despite this it was a period of prolific output; writing being one of the few activities he could manage when he was confined to bed. In these years he wrote some of his most enduring fiction, notably *Treasure Island* (1883), *Kidnapped* (1886), *The Strange Case of Dr Jekyll and Mr Hyde* (1886), and *The Black Arrow* (1888). The circumstances surrounding the creation of *Treasure Island* have become part of literary mythology (see p. 28).

The South Pacific and Samoa

Diagnosed with tuberculosis, Stevenson spent time travelling to find a climate that would suit his health. In 1889, after the death of his father, he went to America and from there embarked on a voyage through the South Pacific, which he wrote about in the articles published collectively as *In The South Seas* (1892). Eventually, the Stevensons settled on Samoa in their dream house, Vailima. The island was well served by mail steamers, which meant that Stevenson could continue writing for serial publication to finance his exile. Here, dinner parties, dances and picnics were held, all of them lively, happy occasions. Stevenson wrote: 'For the first time, I find myself a landholder and a farmer . . . the work seizes and enthrals me.'

But Samoa was not a peaceful idyll; political problems and near warfare set England, America and Germany at odds. Samoan chiefs were imprisoned for objecting to a foreign takeover and Stevenson took an active part, giving aid to the Samoan cause. The Samoans responded with profound gratitude, and Stevenson, known as 'Tusitala, the Teller of Tales', became a revered member of their community. When he died unexpectedly of a brain haemorrhage in 1894, 40 Samoan chiefs bore his body to its final resting place on the summit of Mount Vaea. His grave bore words that he had penned himself:

> Here he lies where he longed to be,
> Home is the sailor, home from the sea,
> And the hunter home from the hill.

Stevenson's last novel, *Weir of Hermiston*, which he was working on until the very day of his death, was unfinished. It was published posthumously in 1896 and many critics believe that had Stevenson been able to complete it, it would have been his finest novel.

National Curriculum reference to this type of work

The Speaking and Listening strand of the National Curriculum for English requires that children have opportunities for group discussion and interaction so that they can investigate, plan and evaluate in a context that allows them to make relevant contributions to the topic of discussion. Reference is also made to the importance of talk for different purposes, including presentation to different audiences. With regard to reading, teachers are directed to help pupils acquire skills, such as scanning and skimming, that will enable them to become efficient researchers and able to obtain specific information through detailed reading.

In researching biographical and autobiographical information, children need to know that subjective opinions are often stated as fact and presented as if the views of the writer are unproblematic. The National Curriculum and NLS draw attention to the 'higher order' reading skill of being able to distinguish fact from opinion.

Specific NLS references

Year 4 Term 1	T19	To understand and use the terms 'fact' and 'opinion'; to begin to distinguish the two in reading and other media.
Year 4 Term 2	T16	To prepare for factual research by reviewing what is known, what is needed, what is available and where one might search.
Year 4 Term 2	T17	To scan texts in print or on screen to locate key words or phrases, useful headings and key sentences and to use these as a tool for summarising text.
Year 5 Term 1	T26	Note making: to fillet passages for relevant information and present ideas which are effectively grouped and linked.
Year 6 Term 1	T11	To distinguish between biography and autobiography; to distinguish between fact, opinion and fiction; to distinguish between implicit and explicit points of view and how these can differ.
Year 6 Term 3	T17	To appraise a text quickly and effectively; to retrieve information from it; to find information quickly and evaluate its value.

Biographical activities

Objectives
- To develop an interest in Robert Louis Stevenson.
- To place Robert Louis Stevenson in his historical and literary context.
- To develop knowledge and understanding of the features of biographical writing and begin to evaluate biographical information through, for example, identifying fact and opinion.
- To conduct independent research into a chosen aspect of Robert Louis Stevenson's life using a range of resources, including the internet.

Outcome
To produce a *PowerPoint* presentation about Robert Louis Stevenson or a short film using a digital multimedia package, such as *Imovie* or *Microsoft Movie Maker*. Ideally, this should be for presentation to an audience, e.g. parents, another class, etc.

Resources
Photocopies of extracts; additional biographical material if required (see resource list).

Introduction
Biographical study is a good starting point for a unit of work focusing on a particular author. It generates interest and curiosity prior to reading the books. If the writer lived at a time or in a place that is significantly different from the children's experiences, such study will help to build the historical, geographical and literary context that can assist appreciation of the books.

A biography is a form of recount, a written exposition and analysis of someone else's life. Most biographies (but not all) are about the lives of eminent people, such as Robert Louis Stevenson. They can be structured to cover the entire life of the subject, from birth to death, but they can also be structured thematically, focusing on key elements of the subject's life (e.g. writing achievements, travels, etc). The process of writing biography has some similarities to the process of writing fiction in as much as the biographer characterises the subject, usually to develop the reader's empathetic response. The best biographies paint lively portraits and present a rounded subject, recognising personal strengths and weaknesses.

A biographer must have a commitment to research – readers expect factual accuracy. However, all biographers will have their own biases about their subjects, and biographies therefore contain both facts and opinions. Recognising that a biography does not provide **the truth** is an important high order reading skill which children can be helped to develop. Sources of information that might be used when researching for a biography include letters, journals, diaries, eyewitness accounts, news reports, interviews, photographs and obituaries.

A biography reconstructs past experience, so it is characteristically written in the past tense, using temporal connectives ('then', 'later') and adverbial clauses of time ('After his father's death . . .'). As biographies tell us about a subject's actions and events, they frequently employ verbs of action (e.g. 'set out', 'abandoned', 'worked').

Teaching sequence
The following shows a suggested outline for teaching a biographical unit of work, based on material about the life of Robert Louis Stevenson. To assist you, some biographical and autobiographical extracts suitable for group work have been reproduced in this book (pp. 15–21), but there is a wealth of material about Robert Louis Stevenson available in book form and on the internet. Much of this material, such as Stevenson's travel writing and collections of letters, is not specifically intended for children, but with careful selection, editing and mediation, it can be made accessible to them. Guided exploration of this material will provide an opportunity to examine language change over time. Pictures and visual references in books published for adults can also be used. The suggested plan lasts for five lessons of one hour with some additional time allowed for independent research. The work could easily be developed over a longer period particularly where historical objectives are incorporated in the planning.

Lesson	Shared work	Group work
1.	Introduce Robert Louis Stevenson. Introduce the biography genre. Shared reading, Photocopiable sheet 1.1.	
2.	Shared reading, Photocopiable sheet 1.2. Compare information. Consider the relevance of the information source.	Find out about Stevenson. Assign research tasks. Use a KWL grid (see p. 9) to construct and identify sources.
3.	Evaluating, reviewing and selecting information. Identify fact and opinion in biographical writing. Recap note-taking.	Gather together information sources. Select texts and search for information. Take notes.
4.	Structure and organise information. Plan the presentation.	Write text. Find images. Edit.
5.	Shared writing. Prepare the *Powerpoint* presentation. Order the information.	Create the presentation.

Lesson 1

Preparation
Gather together a collection of Stevenson's books and related material, such as film posters, video inserts, postcards, a street map of Edinburgh, information books, maps and brochures about the areas of France that Stevenson visited, Samoa, California, etc. and create a stimulus display before starting the unit of work (see resource list p. 91). Invite children to contribute to the display (they may already have illustrated versions of Stevenson's books or film merchandise).

Shared work
Introduce the children to one of Stevenson's books. Talk about the features of the book that you particularly enjoyed. Ask the children if they have heard of the author and whether they know of any other books written by him. Briefly talk about any film adaptations that they know. You might want to tell them that they will be studying an adaptation in depth later on.

Explain to the class that they are going to be learning about Robert Louis Stevenson and will be working towards the preparation of a multimedia presentation.

Before reading Photocopiable sheet 1.1 (p. 15), explain that it is taken from the biography of Robert Louis Stevenson printed in the Puffin Classics edition of his novel *Kidnapped*. Look at the morphology of the word bio + graph + y. Ask the children if they can work out a definition: 'bio' (life), 'graph' (write), 'y' (suffix denoting the word class – noun).

Show where biographies can be located in the school library and explain how they are shelved in the local public library (i.e. often in a separate section organised alphabetically according to subject rather than by the author's surname). Ask the children if they ever choose to read biographies. Why? Why not? Perhaps they know an adult who likes reading biographies and can be encouraged to talk to them about their choice of reading material.

Read the extract. Invite the children to talk about anything they found interesting or puzzling and clarify any unfamiliar vocabulary using a dictionary as appropriate.

Paired work
In pairs, ask the children to reread the extract and jot down in bullet form anything new that they learnt about Stevenson from this short biography. Ask them to share their views about the kind of person they imagine Robert Louis Stevenson to be.

Lesson 2

Shared work

Briefly recap what the class has already learnt about Robert Louis Stevenson. Ask the children what they would expect to find in a recount of someone's life and make a list (e.g. personal details, lasting contribution, information about the person's thoughts, ideas, beliefs, the views of others who knew them, etc).

Tell the children that the source of Photocopiable sheet 1.2 is The Stevenson House Website. This is the house in Edinburgh where Stevenson lived from early childhood. Today it is used as a venue for receptions, recitals and other events. Distribute copies and read the sheet aloud to the class. Discuss any aspect that the children found interesting or puzzling and clarify the meaning of any unknown vocabulary, e.g. 'meteorological purgatory'.

Does the source of the biography have any bearing on the information that has been selected? Reread paragraph 3 and ask the children to identify words and phrases that show how the selection of content is related to the purpose of this particular biographical source (there is a clear focus on Edinburgh and the house). Draw attention to characteristic features of biographical writing that are evident in the text (see p. 5).

Group work

Explain the task. In small groups, pupils are going to use a range of resources, including the internet, to further research the life and achievements of Robert Louis Stevenson. Assign different research tasks to groups or provide a list of suggestions for the groups to select from. Suggested group tasks:

1. Using reference texts, including a biographical dictionary and internet sources, construct a timeline of Stevenson's life. Include significant historical events on the timeline, e.g. important events in Scottish and British history, world of literature, scientific inventions. The group might be given a blank or partially completed timeline to complete (with significant events in Stevenson's life). An example of a timeline is provided on Photocopiable sheet 1.3, but the group may select different events.

2. Investigate Stevenson's childhood using selected biographical extracts and poems from *A Child's Garden of Verses*. 'The Land of Counterpane' (Photocopiable sheet 1.4 and accompanying prompts) draws on his experience of having to occupy himself when unwell. Other useful examples include 'Unseen Playmate', 'Bed in Summer', 'Escape at Bedtime' and 'To Alison Cunningham'.

3. Find out about the books that Stevenson enjoyed reading. *Coral Island, The Last of the Mohicans, The Pilgrim's Progress, The Three Musketeers* and *King Lear* are all mentioned in his essays and other writings. In an essay entitled 'My First Book: *Treasure Island*, Stevenson cites *Robinson Crusoe, Masterman*

Ready and Washington Irving's *Tales of a Traveller* as antecedents of *Treasure Island*. Gather together copies of the books he is known to have enjoyed and read blurbs. Find out further information from reference sources.

4. Research Stevenson's travels in France and Belgium using selected extracts from his travel book, *An Inland Voyage,* and from biographical sources.
5. Research Stevenson's travels in the Massif Central using extracts from his travel book, *Travels with a Donkey*, and from biographical sources.
6. Gather together information about Stevenson's novels and the contexts of their writing, using book blurbs, biographical extracts and video reference material.
7. Find out about Stevenson's South Sea travels, life on Samoa and his house at Valima using extracts from biographical sources, letters (Photocopiable sheets 1.5 and 1.6, and accompanying prompts) and images from the internet (see resource list p. 91). Travel guides, such as Michelle Bennett (2003) *Lonely Planet: Samoan Islands*, will provide an overview of the history, culture and politics.
8. Investigate contemporary evaluations of Stevenson's life using obituary sources (Photocopiable sheet 1.7 and accompanying prompts). Some of the biographies listed above have extracts from obituaries and some newspaper archives can be accessed online.
9. Research Stevenson's lasting contribution to children's literature by searching for information about film adaptations, sequels and different illustrated versions of his *Child's Garden of Verses*, etc. (see resource list p. 91). The internet is a very good place to find film and book reviews.

Introduce, or recap, the use a KWL grid as a means of focusing research.

What we already KNOW	What we WANT to find out	What we have LEARNED

Ask each group to complete the first two columns of a KWL grid related to their area of investigation. When they have done this, ask them to produce a list of possible sources of information to help with their enquiry.

Plenary
Review and evaluate each group's plans. Encourage the children to think critically about their questions, especially whether they are likely to be able to find the answers. Guide them to sources of information that they have not considered.

Lesson 3
Shared work
Ask the children to consider whether a biography tells the truth about someone's life. Discuss the difference between **fact** and **opinion**. Explain that a biography is dependent on factual information but it is also likely to include some of the writer's personal opinion. Reread the third paragraph of Photocopiable sheet 1.2 and ask the children to find one statement that is a fact and one statement that is the opinion of the writer. Explain that if a statement is an opinion it does not necessarily make it **untrue**.

Strategy check:

- Ask each group to briefly review their questions and outline the resources they will be using.
- Review their research skills, e.g. skimming, scanning, reading to find detail.
- Remind the children about the key principles of note-taking (e.g. noting main ideas). Suggest that they might want to write down interesting quotations (e.g. interesting things said by or about Stevenson).

Group work
- Using a range of resources, find answers to the questions generated.
- Make notes of key points.
- Write down interesting quotations and keep a record of the source.
- Take copies of images that might be used in the presentation.

Plenary
- Review the information gathered.
- How easy/difficult was the task? Why?
- Are there any unanswered questions? Where might the answers be found?

Lesson 4
Shared work
Further distinguish between factual evidence and the opinion of the writer. Ask groups to identify one fact and one opinion that they have discovered about Stevenson. Share and evaluate each other's suggestions.

Explain that the next group task is to organise their contribution to the *PowerPoint* presentation and to write the text. Distribute a planner showing six blank slides (Photocopiable sheet 1.8). Explain that each group needs to decide which images and text to use on each of the slides. Some groups may not need six slides and others may need more.

Shared writing
Use a prepared blank slide to show how information in note form can be used to make a *PowerPoint* slide. If available, use an interactive whiteboard to demonstrate this task; alternatively use a flip chart or whiteboard.

Group work
- Order the information.
- Decide on text and images that will go on each slide.
- Draw or scan the images as required.
- Write the text.

Plenary
Review and evaluate. Ask the children to think about the ordering of the information and the appropriateness of the image and text selected.

Lesson 5

Shared work
Introduce or recap the use of *PowerPoint*. Using the piece of shared writing from the previous lesson, show how this can be presented on a slide. Consider three different alternatives, using different colours, fonts and layout. Discuss which is the easiest to read, which suits the subject matter, etc. Explain that the task is to translate their plans into a *PowerPoint* presentation that is readable and demonstrates sensitivity for the material. So while they might have personal preferences for candyfloss pink or psychedelic circle patterns, these might not be the best choices for a biographical presentation about Robert Louis Stevenson!

Group work
- Create the *PowerPoint* presentation using sympathetic design and layout of text and image.
- Add the slide transitions.
- Make judicious selection of sound effects.

Plenary
- Review and evaluate the presentations.
- Merge the groups' work to create one large presentation; decide which order to put the presentations in.
- Make arrangements for showing the presentation to parents, another class, in assembly, etc.

Extract notes

Biography 3

'Land of Counterpane' is one of the poems in *A Child's Garden of Verses* that draws on Stevenson's childhood experience.

Key words

leaden soldiers:	Toy soldiers used to be made of lead. Lead is a soft metal and is toxic so it is no longer used in the manufacture of toys.
drills:	training for soldiers; involves learning how to march, turn, handle arms
dale:	a valley
plain:	level, flat land
counterpane:	cover for a bed

Prompts
- Read the poem. Were there any words or phrases that you didn't understand?
- Does this poem remind you of anything that has happened to you? In what ways are your experiences similar to those of the child in the poem? In what ways are your experiences different?
- Create an illustration for the poem. Use reference materials to help with period detail, e.g. Mandy Ross (2004), *Life in the Past: Victorian Toys*, Heinemann

Biography 4

This extract is taken from a longer essay written by Andrew Lang. Lang was a personal friend of Stevenson and a fellow Scot who is best remembered for his collections of folktales, *The Blue Fairy Book*, *The Brown Fairy Book*, *The Crimson Fairy Book*, etc. In his time he was a popular journalist, writing for *The Daily News*. In the extract he describes his first, somewhat less than favourable impression of Stevenson. The rest of the essay from which this is taken gives an appraisal of Stevenson's writing.

Key words

Mentone:	a town on the French/Italian border, frequented in Stevenson's time by literati and artists
Tyrolese hat:	fashionable headgear originating from the Austrian Tyrol, often decorated with feathers
celerity:	quick changing
innocent impeachment:	light-hearted accusation
aesthetic:	an affected code of behaviour, style and appearance
nous autres:	French for 'the rest of us'

Prompts
- After reading the text, discuss what interested you. Did you find anything puzzling or surprising?
- Find out about Andrew Lang, using a biographical dictionary (e.g. *Chambers Biographical Dictionary*), dictionary of literature or an internet search. Find out what you can about his friendship with Robert Louis Stevenson.
- Read the passage. Identify words or phrases that are unfamiliar and check their meaning. Reread the passage.
- Highlight words and phrases that show that Lang's first impression of Stevenson WAS NOT favourable in one colour. Choose a second colour and highlight words and phrases that suggest that Lang's first impression of Stevenson WAS favourable. Summarise Lang's first impressions in your own words.

After reading the passage, draw an image of Stevenson. Search the internet and other bibliographic sources for real images of Stevenson. Do these images match your expectations?

Biography 5

Thomas Archer was the son of Stevenson's friend William Archer and there are several examples of the correspondence to him in *Pacific Voyages*. Stevenson playfully addresses his young correspondent as Tomarcher. The letter was written after the Stevensons set sail from America before they made their new home at Vailima, Samoa. In this letter Stevenson mentions those observations that he thinks will interest and amuse his young friend.

Key words

Virgil's *Aeneid*/ Latin Dictionary — Books that would have been familiar texts to all Victorian schoolboys.

Skerryvore — Skerryvore lighthouse, built in 1844 by Stevenson's uncle, Alan Stevenson (1807–65), was considered by the Institute of Civil Engineers to be 'the finest combination of mass with elegance to be met within architectural or engineering structures'. Stevenson wrote two poems about the lighthouse: 'Skerryvore' and 'Skerryvore: the parallel' (published in *Underwoods*). Tom Archer's father, William Archer, had written about Stevenson's idealised vision of the lighthouse some years earlier and the two had exchanged a correspondence. Stevenson's House in Bournemouth was also called Skerryvore.

Skerryvore
For love of lovely words, and for the sake
Of those, my kinsmen and my countrymen,
Who early and late in the windy ocean toiled

To plant a star for seamen, where was then
The surfy haunt of seals and cormorants:
I, on the lintel of this cot, inscribe
The name of a strong tower.

impudent	cheeky
prodigal	wasteful, extravagant
bonnet	straw or cloth hat held in place by ribbons tied under the chin
charter	in this instance, to hire

Prompts
- Read the letter. Does this text remind you of anything else you have read? Did it remind you of anything that has happened to you?
- Was there anything that you found puzzling or surprising in this passage?
- Can you identify at least one opinion that Stevenson expresses about the island of Tahiti?
- In a different colour, highlight any words or phrases that suggest Stevenson is sharing a joke with his young friend.

Having read this letter, jot down some words that you think describe Robert Louis Stevenson's personality.

Biography 6

Key words

obituary	published death notice and brief biography
dispatch	a written message sent in haste
apoplexy	a stroke
keenest	most sharply or strongly
Pall Mall Gazette	an evening newspaper founded in 1865
Westminster Gazette	a daily newspaper founded in 1893

Prompts
- Read the obituary. Was there anything you found interesting about this piece? Was there anything you found puzzling?
- Highlight the parts of the text that give the factual notice of Stevenson's death.
- Highlight at least one opinion about Stevenson.
- Highlight any facts that you did not previously know about Stevenson.
- In a different colour identify and highlight a quotation. What does the quotation mean?
- Find Paa Mountain on a map of Samoa.
- What impression do you get of Stevenson from this obituary?

Biography 1

Robert Louis Stevenson (1850–94) was born into a famous Edinburgh engineering family. His middle name was originally Lewis, but Robert changed the spelling, while keeping the pronunciation. His father wanted him to become an engineer, but Robert's constant ill health pushed him towards an indoor job.

He studied law and was called to the Scottish Bar in 1875; but he made little effort as a lawyer, since he was already trying to make his mark in the world of literature. He published a number of essays and articles and accounts of his travels: he travelled widely all his life, in search of a climate that suited him. Success eluded him, however, until 1883 when *Treasure Island* was published.

With his emphasis on character as well as on plot, Stevenson created a revolution in the writing of adventure stories and several of his most famous books fall into this genre. *Kidnapped* (which was first published in 1886) is an outstanding example. Stevenson was well versed in Scottish.

From the introduction to *Kidnapped*, Puffin Classics (1994)

Biography 2

The Stevenson House was the childhood home of Robert Louis Stevenson (1850–94), creator of *Treasure Island, Kidnapped* **and** *Jekyll and Hyde,* **from the age of six until he finally left in 1880.**

Born in Edinburgh in 1850, the son of Thomas Stevenson a noted lighthouse engineer, Robert Louis Stevenson grew up in the Stevenson House at 17 Heriot Row from the age of six. Here he was cared for through many illnesses by his mother and his beloved nurse Alison Cunningham, known as 'Cummie', whom he described in the Dedication of his collection of poems for children, *A Child's Garden of Verses*, as 'My second mother, my first wife'. Prevented by ill-health from going much to ordinary schools, the Stevenson House was the centre of his world, and his mind was nourished by ceaseless reading as well as the stories told by Cummie of ghosts, ghouls, Scottish history and the Bible. He also travelled with his father around Scotland on his engineering business – once descending in a complete diving suit of brass helmet, lead boots, etc. to view the underwater works for the harbour at Wick, in northern Scotland – as well as journeying with his parents to the Continent.

Intended by his father to be trained as a civil engineer, RLS matriculated to the University of Edinburgh in 1867. It was soon clear, however, that the young man was unsuited for the work and he agreed with his father to study law, to give him a steady income should writing – already his chosen path – fail him. Literature, however, had seized him. Edinburgh and the Stevenson House were still his home, and the centre of his imagination, but he began to travel more and further. London, Bournemouth, France and the Continent all drew him – for his health and sheer wanderlust. Ever and again, however, he came back to Edinburgh, that 'meteorological purgatory' (*Edinburgh Picturesque Notes*) and this house.

On one of his voyages to France, he met his future wife, Fanny Vandergrift Osborne, and her family in an artists' colony near Paris. Stricken by his passion for her he followed her when she returned to her home in California, and the couple was married at San Francisco in 1880. They travelled together to Europe shortly afterwards, and lived variously at London, Bournemouth, Davos and elsewhere, the locations more and more dictated by RLS's health. Poems, articles, reviews and novels were written in these years.

After his father's death in 1887, and because his poor health could no longer tolerate a European climate, in 1888 RLS finally abandoned Britain as a home and set out on wanderings that saw him and his family eventually wash up on the shores of the Samoan islands, having covered vast areas of the Pacific in small sailing ships. He worked hard and long at his craft, that 'worm that never sleeps' – conscience – driving him on to his more mature work, which as he died was left unfinished in *Weir of Hermiston*, which just might have been his best novel yet.

From the Stevenson House website http://www.stevenson-house.co.uk/rls.htm

PHOTOCOPIABLE SHEET 1.3

Timeline

Date	Robert Louis Stevenson	National and world events
1850	Born in Edinburgh.	
1853	Stevenson family move to Heriot Row.	Compulsory vaccination against smallpox.
1854		The Crimean War begins. Charles Dickens's *Hard Times* published.
1856		Crimean War ends.
1857		Indian Mutiny.
1859		Charles Darwin's *On the Origin of the Species* published. Kenneth Grahame, author of *The Wind in the Willows*, born in Edinburgh. Arthur Conan Doyle, author of *Sherlock Holmes*, born in Edinburgh. National Gallery of Scotland opens in Edinburgh.
1861		Death of Prince Albert. Hans Christian Andersen's *Fairy Tales* published.
1863		William Booth forms Salvation Army.
1865		Lewis Carroll's *Alice's Adventures in Wonderland* published.
1867	Matriculates to Edinburgh University.	Lister pioneers antiseptic surgery in Edinburgh. The first typewriter is invented.
1869		Cutty Sark built at Dumbarton. Sophia Jex-Blake the first female British medical student studies in Edinburgh. Suez Canal opens.
1871		Stanley finds Livingstone in Africa.
1872		Scottish Education Act. First international football match is played at Queen's Park between England and Scotland.
1873		Blue jeans patented by Levi-Strauss in USA.
1875	Passes law exams and is called to the bar.	
1876	Meets Fanny Osborne. Canoe trip to France and Belgium.	Alexander Graham Bell invents the telephone.
1877		Thomas Edison invents the first records.
1878	*An Inland Voyage* published. *Edinburgh Picturesque Notes* published. Cevennes trip through France's Massif Central with his donkey Modestine.	Joseph Swan demonstrates new electric lights in Newcastle, England. Tay rail bridge opens.
1879	*Travels With a Donkey* published. Stevenson sails to America hoping to persuade Fanny to marry him.	Thomas Edison invents the light bulb in the USA. Tay Bridge disaster – collapses into the river.
1880	Stevenson marries Fanny in San Francisco and they return to Scotland.	
1881	Stevenson writes *Treasure Island* after creating a treasure map with his stepson Lloyd.	Natural History Museum opens in London.
1883	*Treasure Island* published. *Silverado Squatters: a sketch from a Californian Mountain* published.	
1885	*A Child's Garden of Verses* published.	
1886	*Kidnapped* published. *The Strange Case of Dr Jekyll and Mr Hyde* published.	Irish Home Rule. Coca-Cola invented in Atlanta, USA. Daimler produce the first motor car.
1887	Stevenson's father dies.	
1888	*Black Arrow* published.	Founding of the Scottish Labour Party by Kier Hardie.
1889	*The Master of Ballantrae* published. Stevensons set sail for the South Pacific.	
1890		First train over the Forth Bridge.
1891		Arthur Conan Doyle's *The Adventures of Sherlock Holmes* published.
1892		Kier Hardie becomes the first Labour MP. Braille typewriter invented.
1893	*Catriona*, the sequel to *Kidnapped*, published.	The zip is patented.
1894	Stevenson dies at Valima on the Island of Samoa.	Rudyard Kipling's *Jungle Book* published.
1895		Marconi's first radio transmission across the Atlantic. Roentgen discovers X-rays.

Biography 3

'Land of counterpane'

When I was sick and lay a-bed,
I had two pillows at my head,
And all my toys beside me lay
To keep me happy all the day.

And sometimes for an hour or so
I watched my leaden soldiers go,
With different uniforms and drills,
Among the bed-clothes, through the hills;

And sometimes sent my ships in fleets
All up and down among the sheets;
Or brought my trees and houses out,
And planted cities all about.

I was the giant great and still
That sits upon the pillow-hill,
And sees before him, dale and plain,
The pleasant land of counterpane.

Robert Louis Stevenson (1885)
A Child's Garden of Verses

Biography 4

He looked as, in my eyes, he always did look, more like a lass than a lad, with a rather long, smooth oval face, brown hair worn at greater length than is common, large lucid eyes, but whether blue or brown I cannot remember, if brown, certainly light brown. On appealing to the authority of a lady, I learn that brown WAS the hue. His colour was a trifle hectic, as is not unusual at Mentone, but he seemed, under his big blue cloak, to be of slender, yet agile frame. He was like nobody else whom I ever met. There was a sort of uncommon celerity in changing expression, in thought and speech. His cloak and Tyrolese hat (he would admit the innocent impeachment) were decidedly dear to him. On the frontier of Italy, why should he not do as the Italians do? It would have been well for me if I could have imitated the wearing of the cloak!

I shall not deny that my first impression was not wholly favourable. 'Here,' I thought, 'is one of your aesthetic young men, though a very clever one.' What the talk was about, I do not remember; probably of books. Mr Stevenson afterwards told me that I had spoken of Monsieur Paul de St Victor, as a fine writer, but added that 'he was not a British sportsman'. Mr Stevenson himself, to my surprise, was unable to walk beyond a very short distance, and, as it soon appeared, he thought his thread of life was nearly spun. He had just written his essay, 'Ordered South', the first of his published works, for his 'Pentland Rising' pamphlet was unknown, a boy's performance. On reading 'Ordered South' I saw, at once, that here was a new writer, a writer indeed; one who could do what none of us, *nous autres*, could rival, or approach.

Extract from *Recollections of Robert Louis Stevenson* by Andrew Lang
Accessed 2nd February 2003
http://mastertexts.com/Lang_Andrew/Adventures_amon_Books/Chapter00002.htm

Biography 5

DEAR TOMARCHER, – This is a pretty state of things! Seven o'clock and no word of breakfast! And I was awake a good deal last night, for it was full moon, and they had made a great fire of cocoa-nut husks down by the sea, and as we have no blinds or shutters, this kept my room very bright. And then the rats had a wedding or a school-feast under my bed. And then I woke early, and I have nothing to read except Virgil's *Aeneid*, which is not good fun on an empty stomach, and a Latin dictionary, which is good for naught, and by some humorous accident, your dear papa's article on Skerryvore. And I read the whole of that, and very impudent it is, but you must not tell your dear papa I said so, or it might come to a battle in which you might lose either a dear papa or a valued correspondent, or both, which would be prodigal. And still no breakfast; so I said 'Let's write to Tomarcher'.

This is a much better place for children than any I have hitherto seen in these seas. The girls (and sometimes the boys) play a very elaborate kind of hopscotch. The boys play horses exactly as we do in Europe; and have very good fun on stilts, trying to knock each other down, in which they do not often succeed. The children of all ages go to church and are allowed to do what they please, running about the aisles, rolling balls, stealing mamma's bonnet and publicly sitting on it, and at last going to sleep in the middle of the floor. I forgot to say that the whips to play horses, and the balls to roll about the church – at least I never saw them used elsewhere – grow ready made on trees; which is rough on toy-shops. The whips are so good that I wanted to play horses myself; but no such luck! My hair is grey, and I am a great, big, ugly man. The balls are rather hard, but very light and quite round. When you grow up and become offensively rich, you can charter a ship in the port of London, and have it come back to you entirely loaded with these balls; when you could satisfy your mind as to their character, and give them away when done with to your uncles and aunts.

I have the honour to be Tomarcher's valued correspondent,

A letter from Robert Louis Stevenson to Thomas Archer, Tautira, Island of Tahiti (November 1888).
Taken from Pacific Voyages, June 1888 – November 1890, Chapter 10
http://www.worldwideschool.org/library/books/lit/literarystudies/TheLettersofRobertLouis-Stevenson

Activity: Investigating classics

Objectives
- To contribute to shared discussion evaluating the claim that Robert Louis Stevenson is a classic author.
- To begin to develop an awareness that labels such as 'classic' are subjective and interpreted differently according to personal values.

Outcomes
Group and class discussion at the end of the unit of work on Robert Louis Stevenson.

Resources
Photocopies of the 'What is a classic book?' sheet (p. 26).

Teacher notes
Children are often urged to read 'classic' books, but their thoughts about what makes a book classic may not have been solicited. It can be revealing to follow Watson's lead and ask children: 'What is a classic?' Do the children ever use the word 'classic'? What does it mean to them? Ask them if they can think of any other contexts where the word 'classic' is used: e.g. classic cars, classic jeans, classic film, classic rock anthems, classic cola, etc. Discuss what the label implies in each instance. Have a look at the range of books in the class or school library that have been included in a 'classic series'. A collection of publicity and advertising material containing the word 'classic' can be gathered and displayed. There are lots of different opinions about the word 'classic' (some of them are reproduced on Photocopiable sheet 2.1) and it is important that children are encouraged to contribute freely without feeling they are searching for the correct answer.

Ask the children to suggest titles that they consider qualify for the accolade 'classic'. Are the titles the same as the ones you would have listed? You might ask the children to independently write three titles before sharing their ideas. This allows them to develop some commitment to their own thoughts before hearing the opinions of others. To follow up, investigate the titles that occur most frequently and consider the reasons behind the choices (e.g. recent release of a new Disney film).

Another interesting question that can be explored is: 'Which new books are likely to be tomorrow's classics?' Again, children can produce personal lists before engaging in shared discussion.

Over a period of time, children can produce short presentations on personal favourite classic texts and multiple copies of the books can be added to the class library for others to read.

At the end of your unit of work on Robert Louis Stevenson, review the question: 'Is Robert Louis Stevenson a classic author?' The snippets produced on Photocopiable sheet 2.1 are good discussion generators. Working in small groups, pupils can consider Stevenson's books in the light of each of these comments as well as their own ideas about the definition of 'classic'. Each group can be asked to reach a decision and to produce a bulleted list of arguments to support or refute the claim. The lists can then be used as a basis for class discussion or debate.

What is a classic book?

'For me the books that matter are the ones I either think I would like to read again, or the ones I know I want to press into someone else's hand immediately.'

Liz Attenborough

'And what exactly is a classic novel? One written to last, written carefully, written with feeling and intelligence . . .'

Terence Blacker

'What is a classic novel? A book that changes your life'.

Sarah Dunant

'My definition of a "classic" novel is one which, through its splendid uses of language and its gifted perceptions into our experience, enthralls its own and succeeding generation.'

Richard Hoggart

'When I was at school, a classic meant a novel that was difficult to read or get into.'

Elizabeth Jennings

'To me "classic" novels are novels that appear on shelves in bookshops under "Classics", and are invariably published in series clearly marked "Classics"'

Roger McGough

'A classic novel means different things to different people.'

Tim Pears

'The booksellers' and publishers' convention used to be that pre-1900 is classic and post-1900 is not.'

Tim Waterstone

'What makes a good classic novel? In my opinion, the main ingredient is a good story well told.'

Alison Weir

All taken from Andrew Holgate & Honor Wilson-Fletcher (eds) (1999), *What Makes a Classic a Classic? The Test of Time*, Waterstone's.

3   *Treasure Island*: Historical context

Background

On first encounter, *Treasure Island* might seem a difficult book; certainly the syntax and the vocabulary are very different to modern phrasing, style and register. But the exciting plot and a cast of colourful characters ensure that the story can be enjoyed as much by children today as it was at the end of the nineteenth century. Good expressive reading aloud, combined with oral storytelling, drama and an introduction to some of the adapted versions of the story will breathe fresh life into this fast moving adventure, providing children with a thrilling literary experience. Furthermore, reading the original text, in whole or part, will provide an insight into language change and an enriched language experience.

Note: all quotations and references are taken from the Puffin Classic edition: Robert Louis Stevenson (1994) *Treasure Island,* London: Puffin.

Synopsis

The story begins at the 'Admiral Benbow' inn. An old sea captain, Billy Bones, turns up looking for a room and in fear of 'the one-legged man'. When Billy collapses and dies from 'thundering apoplexy' (after Blind Pew gives him the 'black spot'), Jim discovers a oilskin-wrapped package in his old sea chest. Jim seeks advice from Squire Trelawney and Doctor Livesey. The Squire realises that the map belonged to the notorious pirate, Captain Flint, and that it shows the location of his famous treasure hoard. He travels to Bristol to secure a ship, *The Hispaniola*, and a crew to sail her.

The ship's captain, Captain Smollett, doubts the trustworthiness of the crew especially the one-legged sea cook, Long John Silver. Jim shrugs off his initial misgivings and develops a fondness for the genial Silver. But later, hidden inside an apple barrel, he overhears Silver leading a plot to mutiny. Jim warns the Squire and Captain of the planned treachery.

Arriving at Treasure Island, the crew are given permission to go ashore, and Jim decides to go with them at the last moment. On the island he encounters Ben Gunn, a mariner marooned by Flint three years earlier. Ben resolves to help Jim. Meanwhile the Captain, Squire and doctor take refuge with the loyal members of the crew in an old stockade that they find on the island and Jim is reunited with them. Silver realises that his plan has been discovered. He approaches the stockade waving the truce flag and attempts to strike a bargain, offering the Captain and his followers safe passage in return for the map. His offer is refused and a battle ensues. Jim escapes from the stockade and, using Ben Gunn's boat, sails out to the *Hispaniola*.

After a fight with the terrifying Israel Hands he takes charge of the ship and heads back to the stockade to find that it has been taken by Silver and his men. Silver tells Jim that he is now on the doctor's side. The next day they set out to find the treasure, but after a hot and exhausting trail they find the chest only to discover that the treasure has gone. A shot is fired from the woods and Livesey appears with Ben Gunn. The pirates beat a hasty retreat. Ben Gunn reveals that he dug up the treasure and took it back to his cave. Silver, still pretending to be on the doctor's side, helps to load the treasure aboard the *Hispaniola*. They take the ship into port to enlist more crew and in the morning Silver has disappeared with some of the treasure. The others return home and Jim swears that he will never again go hunting for treasure.

Context of writing

Treasure Island is a book that has been enjoyed by both adults and children before the notion of the 'crossover' book was invented. Stevenson referred to *Treasure Island* as 'My first Book', even though he had already published several volumes of travel writing. In an essay, he wrote: 'It was far indeed from being my first book, for I am not a novelist alone. But I am well aware that my paymaster, The Great Public, regards what else I have written with indifference, if not aversion . . . When I am asked to talk of my first book, no question in the world but what is meant is my first novel' (*The Art of Writing and Other Essays*).

Robert Louis Stevenson started writing *Treasure Island* in 1881 at the instigation of his 12-year-old stepson Lloyd Osborne. One rainy day, while they were on holiday in Braemar, Scotland, Stevenson occupied Lloyd by drawing a treasure map, which prompted Lloyd to suggest how wonderful it would be to have a story about it. The map served as the inspiration: ' . . . as I paused upon my map of "Treasure Island", the future characters of the book began to appear there visibly among imaginary woods; and their brown faces and bright weapons peeped out upon me from unexpected quarters, as they passed to and fro, fighting and hunting treasure, on those few square inches of a flat projection. The next thing I knew I had some papers before me and was writing a list of Chapters' (*The Art of Writing and Other Essays*).

Each day, Stevenson sat by the fireside composing his story, and in the afternoon he would read it aloud to his father and stepson. Stevenson's father greatly admired the story: 'I had counted on one boy, I found I had two in my audience. My father caught fire at once with all the romance and childishness of his original nature' (*The Art of Writing and Other Essays*). In fact his father was so taken with the story that he became a collaborator in its creation: 'When the time came for Billy Bones's chest to be ransacked, he must have passed the better part of the day preparing, on the back of a legal envelope, an inventory of its contents, which I exactly followed; and the name of "Flint's old ship" the Walrus was given at his particular request' (*The Art of Writing and Other Essays*).

Some of the incidents in the book were based on incidents in Stevenson's life. The episode when Jim overhears the crew conspiring to mutiny is based on an incident that Stevenson's father recalled from childhood when he had overheard a similar conspiracy against *his* father.

Originally called *The Sea Cook,* the story first appeared in 17 instalments in *Young Folks* magazine between 1881–82; the title was changed by the magazine's editor. But it wasn't until it was published as an adult novel in 1883 that *Treasure Island* was established as a success.

Historical context

Stevenson does not specify the year that *Treasure Island* is set. Jim Hawkins starts his narration, 'I take up my pen in the year of grace 17–'. It is most likely that the story is set at the beginning of the eighteenth century, when British piracy was at its height. It was a period when notorious pirate characters, such as Edmund Teach and Blackbeard, sailed the Atlantic, Indian and Caribbean oceans. In those days, piracy was a significant threat to a maritime power like Britain, a country dependent on sea trade for political and economic power. By the 1730s, the British navy was powerful enough to reduce the threat posed by piracy. At the time Stevenson wrote *Treasure Island,* piracy belonged to the distant past, but romantic tales of swashbuckling mariners were appealing in a period when sail power was steadily and convincingly being overtaken by steam power.

Literary context

Victorian children's literature was predominantly didactic, written to educate child readers with its moral messages. The publication of Lewis Carroll's *Alice's Adventures in Wonderland* (1865) is credited as a landmark in the history of children's literature, being written first and foremost to entertain and delight. Although *Treasure Island* does convey some moral message – Jim learns about responsibility, resourcefulness and courage – it is most memorable for its story and colourful characterisation; entertainment is, without a doubt, privileged over instruction.

Genre

Treasure Island is a sea adventure, a genre which during the nineteenth century enjoyed enormous popularity. Naval tales told of the exploits of strong, capable officers in realistic and historical situations. And desert island romances featured shipwrecked or marooned characters. There had been a growth in desert island stories or 'robinsonnades' since the publication of Daniel Defoe's *Robinson Crusoe* in 1719, but the genre was at the height of its popularity at the beginning of the nineteenth century. Over time, the stories changed to reflect the values and beliefs of the time in which they were written. J. D. Wyss's *The Swiss Family Robinson* (1812) is the story of a family who set sail to a new land in search of a better life, but after they are shipwrecked on a desert island establish their home there. The paternalistic family is guided by the authoritarian moral direction of the father. *Masterman Ready* (1841) by Captain Marryat is a realistic depiction of a family on a deserted island. R. M. Ballantyne's *The Coral Island* (1858) is an idealistic story of three youths stranded on an idyllic south sea island, where the only threat comes from a band of pirates. Stevenson was certainly very familiar with these stories and pays tribute to them in his own writing:

On a chill September morning, by the cheek of a brisk fire, and the rain drumming on the window, I began *The Sea Cook*, for that was the original title. I have begun (and finished) a number of other books, but I cannot remember to have sat down to one of them with more complacency. It is not to be wondered at, for stolen waters are proverbially sweet . . . No doubt the parrot once belonged to Robinson Crusoe. No doubt the skeleton is conveyed from Poe. I think little of these, they are trifles and details; and no man can hope to have a monopoly of skeletons or make a corner in talking birds. The stockade, I am told, is from *Masterman Ready*. It may be, I care not a jot. These writers had fulfilled the poet's saying: departing, they had left behind the 'footprints on the sands of time' . . . It is my debt to Washington Irving that exercises my conscience, and justly so, for I believe plagiarism was rarely carried farther. I chanced to pick up the *Tales of a Traveller* some years ago with a view to an anthology of prose narrative. Billy Bones, his chest, the company in the parlour, the whole inner spirit, and a good deal of the material detail of my first Chapters all were there, all were the property of Washington Irving.

Some modern examples of the genre are given in the *Treasure Island* section of the resource list (p. 92).

National Curriculum reference to this type of work

Studying the representation of characters through image analysis provides opportunities for children to engage with aspects of the National Curriculum that require them to evaluate ideas and themes that broaden perspectives and extend thinking. In order to consider how a subject is represented they will need to look for meaning beyond the literal. And in relating their new understanding to previous experience and in comparing representations they will draw on knowledge of other texts they have read.

Specific NLS references

Year 4 Term 1	**T2**	To identify the main characteristics of key characters, drawing on the text; to justify views.
Year 4 Term 2	**T9**	To recognise how certain types of texts are targeted at particular readers; to identify intended audience.
Year 5 Term 1	**T5**	To understand dramatic conventions, including how character can be communicated in words and gesture; to investigate how characters are presented, referring to the text.
Year 5 Term 2	**T9**	To investigate the features of different fiction genres.
Year 6 Term 1	**T4**	To look at connections and contrasts in the work of different writers.
Year 6 Term 1	**T5**	To contribute constructively to shared discussion about literature, responding to and building on the views of others.

Treasure Island activities: Context

Objectives
To begin to analyse the visual representation of character, taking account of purpose, intended audience and response.

Outcome
Display of pirate images from fictional and factual sources with children's analysis of the images.

Resources
Images of pirates (see *Treasure Island* resource list, p. 92); drawing materials; photocopies of image analysis prompt sheet (p. 33).

Representations of pirates
The popular image of the pirate owes a lot to Stevenson's portrayal of the one-legged Long John Silver and Captain Flint's fearsome crew. Since the publication of *Treasure Island*, the pirate has become a popular character in children's books, comics and films, from Captain Hook in J.M. Barrie's *Peter Pan* to *Captain Pugwash*. Much recent historical work has sought to look at the relationship between fact and fiction in the depiction of pirates. Through studying images of pirates, children can be encouraged to consider different levels of 'reality'. They can look at the extent to which representation is influenced by genre, e.g. a children's comic might show characters being marched along a gang plank and eaten by sharks, whereas a U certificated live action film aimed at the same audience will not. Crucially, children can relate images to discussions about the intended audience (e.g. Captain Pugwash is popular with the under fives and Captain Teachum will be more appreciated by children in KS2). They should also develop an awareness that different audiences will respond differently to the images – for instance, stereotypical pirate images have been criticised on the grounds that disability is associated with unpleasant and immoral characteristics. With regard to stereotyping, children should be able to argue for more realistic representations where this is appropriate, at the same time recognising that the use of stereotype can provide a pleasurable reading experience.

You might start by providing a range of drawing materials and asking the children to draw what they think a pirate should look like. Tell the children to draw what is in their head and not to worry about what other children are drawing. Share the images, focusing on the similarities and differences. Where have these images come from? From books, films, comics? A variation of this activity is to make a physical image of a pirate. In small groups, the children sculpt a volunteer into an image they think represents a pirate. They can be guided to extend their work by considering where the eyes should look, expression, gesture and posture.

Image analysis: fictional pirates
Find a range of pirate images. Look in books available in the school and class library. Use the resource list on p. 91. Invite the children to bring images from home. Collect images from books, comics and from film merchandising. Give pairs an image of a pirate and ask them to analyse the image using Photocopiable sheet 3.1 to aid their discussion.

Image analysis: factual sources
Now allocate each pair an image of a pirate from a historical source. Ask the students to note the similarities and differences between the fictional and information images.

Similarities	Differences

Class discussion
Consider how closely the fictional and factual sources represent the reality of pirates. Guide the children to consider whether an image presented in a factual text is necessarily closer to 'reality' than one from a fictional source.

PHOTOCOPIABLE SHEET 3.1

Pirates: Image analysis

Choose three words to describe this picture.	
What do you think you are supposed to feel when you see this image?	
Where would you expect to find this image? Why?	
Who do you think is the intended audience for this picture? How can you tell?	
How do the style of the drawing and the materials used contribute to the overall impression?	
What does each of the following contribute to the overall impression?	
• Expression	
• Gesture	
• Hairstyle	
• Clothes	
• Accessories (parrots, telescopes, etc.)	

Activity: Book display – antecedents and sequels

Objectives
To look at the connections and contrasts in the work of different authors.

Outcome
Display of books showing titles that influenced the writing of *Treasure Island* and those that have been inspired by it.

Resources
Using biographical sources and the resource list (p. 91), gather together copies of the books that directly influenced Stevenson (e.g. *Robinson Crusoe*, *Coral Island*, etc). Also collect together copies of books that have been inspired by *Treasure Island* and categorise them as:

- books inspired by *Treasure Island* (e.g. J. M. Barrie's *Peter Pan*)
- same genre (e.g. Faulkener's *Moonfleet*)
- sequels (e.g. *Silver's Revenge*, *Jim Hawkins and the Curse of Treasure Island*)
- illustrated versions
- adaptations
- film merchandising.

The children can be encouraged to read the displayed books and to write reviews that can either be added to the display or loosely inserted in the books to aid book selection.

4 *Treasure Island*: Narrative structure and plot

Background

Treasure Island is a quest story with a circular structure: beginning at home, moving away and ultimately returning home. The story has three narrative sections distinguished by setting:

1. The action at the 'Admiral Benbow' serves to set the quest in motion. In the exposition, normality of life at the inn is broken by the arrival of Billy Bones, followed by the pirates, Black Dog and Blind Pew. This section ends with the discovery and identification of the treasure map. Squire Trelawney, Doctor Livesey and Jim Hawkins leave behind their old roles as they prepare for new ones in the quest for Treasure Island.
2. Aboard the *Hispaniola* the mood is that of a romantic adventure; it is characterised by optimism and anticipation. Jim eagerly anticipates the voyage and arrival at the island: 'I might have been twice as weary, yet I would not have left the deck; all was so new and interesting to me – the brief commands, the shrill note of the whistle, the men bustling to their places in the glimmer of the ship's lanterns' (p. 81). There is a brief warning of treachery that is to come (p. 87) and Captain Smollett provides a cautionary note, but Jim and the rest of the crew are in good spirits.
3. As the *Hispaniola* nears her destination, the mood changes. The pivotal moment occurs when Jim overhears the mutineers' plot while he is hidden in the apple barrel. The island is a savage place and Jim's description of his first impressions show that it is not what he had expected (see Photocopiable sheet 7.1 (p. 69)).
4. In addition, a short narrative frame is constructed around the story. The book ends, as it begins, as a recollection. In the first paragraph Jim explains how he has been asked to write down the adventure. The closing paragraphs provide some reflection and evaluation of character.

An overview of the structure is presented on page 37 (this table provides an example response to the second activity). We can also distinguish between the **rising action** (the part of the story where the tension builds, between the inciting moment and the climax) and the **falling action** (from the denouement through to the end of the story). A plot line showing the rising and falling action can be drawn like this (see overleaf):

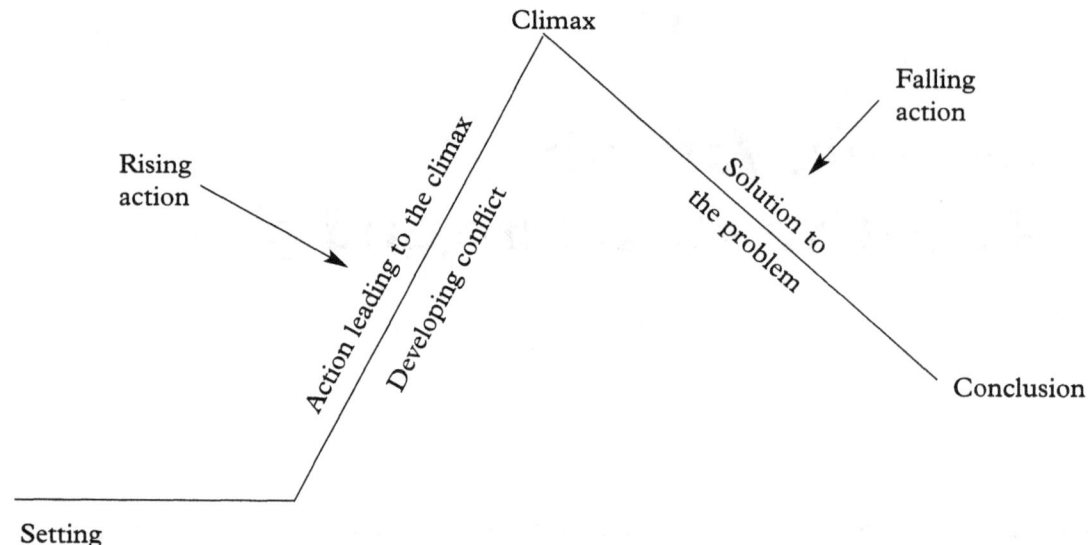

Diagram showing standard narrative presentation.

Repeating cycles of less intense rising and falling action can occur within the development of the story.

The narrative structure of individual Chapters can also be analysed. Originally published in serial form, many Chapters have cliff-hanger endings, pushing the narrative forward to keep readers eager to buy the next instalment. For example, Chapter 4, 'The Sea Chest', ends with Jim and his mother in obvious danger: 'So there we had to stay – my mother almost entirely exposed, and both of us within earshot of the inn' (p. 37). Readers are left on tenterhooks until the following Chapter to find out if, and how, they escape. Other good examples of cliff-hangers occur at the end of Chapter 10, where Jim climbs inside the apple barrel (see Photocopiable sheet 4.2 p. 44), and at the end of Chapter 17.

Stevenson carefully builds suspense throughout the novel. One device is the use of cues to foreshadow future events, e.g. Billy Bones' warning about the one-legged man, Captain Smollett's unease about the crew, Ben Gunn's assertion that he is 'a rich man'. And in Chapter 17 the reader is alerted by references to fire that that all is not well in the Squire's camp.

Another way in which suspense is built and maintained is through the interplay of knowledge and ignorance. The reader is aware of Silver's intentions before Jim overhears the mutinous plot. Later, Jim tells the Squire and Captain of the plans to take the ship but Silver remains unaware that he has been discovered.

There are moments of surprise as well. This is handled particularly well when Stevenson switches the narration from Jim to Dr Livesey and then back again to Jim. This means that the reader is only aware of one side of the story and therefore surprised to find that Jim is captured by Silver on his return to the stockade.

National Curriculum reference to this type of work

The following activities focus on the development of plot and narrative of *Treasure Island* (En2), using drama as a means of exploration structure, thus addressing the National Curriculum requirements for children to participate in a range of drama activities. Through the creation of tableaux, they will use narrative to convey story. Children should be encouraged to evaluate their own and others' contribution and be guided towards quality in their drama work. The suggested outline of work includes a performance element, and children can be taught how to evaluate their contribution to the overall effectiveness of the performance (En1). The opportunity for writing provides an imaginative experience through which children can explore feelings and ideas, focusing on the creative uses of language (En3).

Specific NLS references

Year 4 Term 1　T4　To explore narrative order: identify and map out the main stages of the story.

Year 5 Term 1　T1　To analyse the features of a good opening.

Year 6 Term 2　T1　To understand aspects of narrative structure, e.g. how Chapters in a book are linked together.

Overview of the structure

Narrative section	Plot summary
Opening. Provides information about time, place and characters. Sometimes called the exposition.	The narrator is recording events at the request of Squire Trelawney and Dr Livesey. Time: 17–. Place: Admiral Benbow inn.
Inciting moment. The point in the story when predictability is disrupted, when it becomes evident that there is a story to be told. Sometimes called the complication.	Billy Bones' arrival at the 'Admiral Benbow'.
Development. This is part of the **rising action** (from the inciting moment through to the climax). Within the development there might be further cycles of rising and falling action.	From the arrival of Billy Bones to the discovery of the treasure map; the hiring of the crew; the voyage to Treasure Island; mutiny; Jim captured and held hostage; the search for the treasure.
Climax. This is the moment where tension is at its most intense.	Discovery that the treasure has been excavated. Jim and Silver face the anger of the other five pirates.
Dénouement. The final event that makes a resolution possible. This is also known as **falling action** (from the climax through to the conclusion or coda).	The revelation that Ben Gunn has stowed the treasure in his cave.
Resolution. Brings the conflict to a satisfactory conclusion.	Treasure is recovered and loaded on board the *Hispaniola*. Silver escapes with part of the treasure.
Coda	Jim's ruminations about the effect that money has had on different characters.

Activity: Design a theme park ride

Objective
To identify the main stages in the story, using dramatic interpretation and key quotations from the text.

Outcome
Treasure Island tableaux for theme park ride to be performed for another class, parents or school.

Resources
Copies of *Treasure Island*; copies of Photocopiable sheet 4.1.

The activities can be carried out in the classroom, but a large space is required if the work is to be performed to an audience.

Teacher notes
You could start by asking the children to share experiences of theme park rides, such as *Pirates of the Caribbean* or *Pinocchio*, where a familiar story is presented as a sequence of tableaux depicting the main events. Explain that you are going to create a *Treasure Island* theme park ride by producing a sequence of tableaux.

Prepare copies of Photocopiable sheet 4.1 and a large version for the whiteboard or flip chart. For less experienced groups, a simpler frame might be used. Explain the terms if they are unfamiliar to the children.

You could model completion of the first two items of the second column as a shared writing activity, sharing your thought processes with the children. The children then work in small groups to complete the entire second column. By limiting the number of moments they can select they have to distil the story, picking out the events that are most significant. Reassemble the class and share the selection of key moments, drawing attention to differences and similarities in the choices. Ask groups to justify their choices. After discussion, come to a collective decision about the most significant parts of the story. Point out that there is more than one correct answer, but that you are reaching a collective decision for the purpose of creating a tableau of the story.

Allocate a different section of the story (excluding the opening and coda) to each group and ask them to construct a freeze frame depicting their allocated moment. Guide them to select the point of greatest dramatic tension, especially if they are working on the developing conflict or the climax. The frozen moment should enable the children to focus intently on feelings, expressions, posture, gesture and on the characters they are representing. More experienced groups can create statues, i.e. images that can be viewed from all angles. Groups that have less drama experience can create photographs, i.e. images that are viewed from the front only. Invite the children to share and evaluate the freeze frames, considering how the images could be further improved, e.g. more appropriate expression, more emphatic use of gesture, picking a more dramatic moment, etc. Working in sequence, ask each group to bring their frame to life for 10 seconds and then refreeze.

You can extend this work further by selecting key quotations to accompany the tableaux. Show the children how to complete the third column by selecting a quotation that encapsulates the moment (see example below). Explain why you have chosen a particular quotation. Alternatively, you might choose two quotations and select the most appropriate one with the class.

Introduction/exposition	Told that narrator is recording events at the request of Squire Trelawney and Dr. Livesey. Time 17–. Place: Admiral Benbow inn.	I take up my pen in the year of grace 17–. And go back to the time my father kept the 'Admiral Benbow inn'.

Once each group has a key quotation for their moment, write it on a large sheet of paper. You might give them copies of selected extracts or relevant page numbers to assist their location of the quotations. In turn, each group can take up the freeze frame position. Place their quotation next to the freeze frame, either on the floor or attached to a wall space. Bring each scene to life for 10 seconds and refreeze as the audience moves around. In bringing the scene to life, the children are able to improvise a short piece of dialogue which will enhance their understanding of characters and relationships. Allow time for reflection, evaluation and improvement.

If possible, present the sequence as a promenade presentation to an audience. To do this, present the scenes in sequential order around the room so that the audience can walk through the sequence of freeze frames, reading the quotations. Bring each frame to life in turn. You might also want to use a narrator to introduce the story by reading the opening paragraph and close it by reading the final paragraphs.

As an alternative to the tableaux promenade, you might want the children to design the ride on paper. In this case they would still work with the narrative structure but would use a storyboard instead of creating freeze frame images. They could add notes about special effects, lighting, etc. to their storyboard of the ride.

Narrative structure

	Details	Key quotation
Exposition (time, place, characters)		
Inciting moment (moment when we know a story is going to happen)		
Development		
Development		
Development		
Climax (where tension is most intense)		
Dénouement Final event makes resolution possible		
Resolution Conflict is resolved		
Conclusion/coda		

Activity: Mood and suspense

Objective
To understand aspects of narrative structure, e.g. how Chapters in a book are linked together, with a particular focus on contrasting moods and cliff-hanger endings.

Outcomes
- Write a Chapter opening to follow on from a cliff-hanger ending.
- Display of mood pictures.

Resources
Copies of Photocopiable sheet 4.2 'Inside the Apple Barrel'.

Lesson notes
Read the passage 'Inside the Apple Barrel' (p. 44). Invite the children to share initial responses. What do they think about the way the Chapter ends? Ask if the Chapter ending reminds them of anything else they have read. Introduce the term 'cliff-hanger' if this is not already known. Ask the children to consider why an author would choose to end a Chapter in this way? Explain publishing context. Explain or find definitions for any unfamiliar vocabulary.

Examine more closely the build up of suspense in the passage. Reread the first paragraph. Ask the children to suggest words that describe how Jim is feeling, e.g. relaxed, calm, hopeful, etc. Identify words or phrases that help to create the mood. For example, 'all my work was over and I was on my way to berth' suggests that Jim's actions are routine, nothing untoward is happening. 'Whistling gently to himself' and 'swish of the sea against the bows' create an impression of calm.

Reread the second paragraph and ask the children whether the mood has changed. If so, how? Identify the point at which the mood changes: 'was on the point of doing so when a heavy man sat down with a clash close by'. The words are heavy and clash/contrast with the calm mood already established. Ask the children to suggest words to describe the mood in the second paragraph. Pick out words or phrases that add to the suspense, e.g. 'trembling and listening'. Guide the children to notice how the long sentences in the second paragraph also add to the build up of tension – there are just three sentences.

Use freeze frames to recreate the contrasting moods in this extract. Choose one of the words suggested for the first paragraph, e.g. 'relaxed'. Ask the children to work in small groups to create a freeze frame that reflects the key word. Note: the freeze frame doesn't have to be related to the content of the passage; images can be abstract or figurative. Now choose one of the words suggested for the mood of the second paragraph and carry out the same activity. Take digital photographs of both images and display them along with a copy of the passage and the key words. You might also want to add other images drawn or painted by the children that reflect the contrasting moods. Samples of colour cut from magazines or paint charts as well as music extracts might also be included to create a multi-sensory display.

Work on the cliff-hanger ending to predict what will happen next in the story. In small groups, ask the children to create a freeze frame showing the moment where Jim writes 'from these dozen words I understood that the lives of all honest men aboard depended upon me alone'. When the groups have created the freeze frames ask them to unfreeze and improvise what happens next. Stop the action and discuss how each group developed the story. Use the improvisations as a basis for writing the opening of the next Chapter.

Activity: Story openings

Objective
To analyse the features of a good opening focusing on the sea adventure genre.

Outcome
Write an opening paragraph for an adventure story.

Resources
Copies of the story openings on Photocopiable sheets 4.3, 4.4 and 4.5.

The story openings are taken from *Treasure Island* and two sequels inspired by Stevenson's novel, Robert Leeson's *Silver's Revenge* and Francis Bryan's *Jim Hawkins and the Curse of Treasure Island*. *Silver's Revenge* is narrated by Tom Carter, who takes up the story some years on. *The Curse of Treasure Island* is narrated by Jim Hawkins, now aged 21.

Whole class discussion
You could start by asking the children to jot down on a piece of paper three things that they consider are needed for a good story opening. This strategy ensures that all children can make a contribution to the discussion. Take suggestions from the class, adding them to a list and discussing reasons for the choices. Read and review the suggested list of 'criteria' with the class.

You might then read the opening of *Treasure Island* and discuss the children's initial responses. Ask them to comment on the effectiveness of the opening and to identify any words or phrases that particularly engage their interest.

Usually, we can tell the type of story we are reading from the first few sentences. If you are just beginning to read *Treasure Island*, you could ask the children what sort of story they think the opening comes from. What clues help them to identify the type of story (genre)? Who do they imagine would want to read more of this story?

Choose one or both of the other story openings and repeat the activity. Ask the children which opening they prefer and ask them to justify their choice. How do they think each of the stories will develop based on the information given in the first paragraphs?

Ask the children to write an opening for an adventure story using some of the features they have identified in the story openings that they have studied.

Inside the apple barrel

Now, just after sundown, when all my work was over and I was on my way to berth, it occurred to me that I should like an apple. I ran on deck. The watch was all forward looking out for the island. The man at the helm was watching the luff of the sail, and whistling away gently to himself; and that was the only sound excepting the swish of the sea against the bows and around the sides of the ship.

In I got bodily into the apple barrel, and found there was scarce an apple left; but sitting down there in the dark, what with the sound of the waters and the rocking movement of the ship, I had either fallen asleep, or was on the point of doing so, when a heavy man sat down with rather a clash close by. The barrel shook as he leaned his shoulders against it, and I was just about to jump up when the man began to speak. It was Silver's voice, and, before I had heard a dozen words, I would not have shown myself for all the world but lay there, trembling and listening, in the extreme of fear and curiosity; for from these dozen words I understood that the lives of all honest men aboard depended upon me alone. (*Treasure Island*, pp. 87–88)

Key words
luff: the forward side of a fore-and-aft sail
helm: the steering gear of a ship – the wheel.
berth: in this instance, a built-in bed or bunk, as on a ship
bows: the front section of a ship

The Old Sea Dog at the 'Admiral Benbow'

Squire Trelawney, Dr Livesey, and the rest of these gentlemen having asked me to write down the whole particulars about Treasure Island, from the beginning to the end, keeping nothing back but the bearings of the island, and that only because there is still treasure not yet lifted, I take up my pen in the year of grace 17__, and go back to the time my father kept the 'Admiral Benbow' inn, and the brown old seaman, with the sabre cut, first took up his lodging under our roof.

I remember him as it were yesterday, as he came plodding to the inn door, his sea-chest following behind him in a hand barrow; a tall, strong, heavy, nut-brown man; his tarry pigtail falling over the shoulders of his soiled blue coat; his hands ragged and scarred, with black, broken nails; and the sabre cut across one cheek, a dirty livid white. I remember him looking round the cove and whistling to himself as he did so, and then breaking out in that old sea-song that he sang so often afterwards:

'Fifteen men on the dead man's chest –

Yo-ho-ho, and a bottle of rum!'

in the high, old tottering voice that seemed to have been tuned and broken at the capstan bars. Then he rapped at the door with a bit of a stick, like a handspike that he carried, and when my father appeared, called roughly for a glass of rum. This, when it was brought to him, he drank slowly, like a connoisseur, lingering on the taste and still looking about him at the cliffs and up at our signboard.

Treasure Island pp. 3–4

A mysterious arrival

It began on the first Sunday of August last year, at another inn, the Royal George up on the heath. I had gone there to await the mail coach. Many of its weekly visits brought from Bristol and farther away articles and goods we had sent for.

The landlord of the Royal George is John Culzean. He was a sound neighbour and good friend to my mother in that time I first went abroad. John is an easy man and I like his company. As I waited, he and I spoke of local things, as neighbours do.

A bugle blew from the hilltop; soon we heard the rattle of wheels coming into the yard. John left me to go out and greet the coachman and I saw something quicken between them. The coachman asked some strong question. John nodded his head and listened for a further moment. Then he pointed, first towards the direction of the distant Admiral Benbow and next indicated me through the open door of his own parlour. I sensed that my name had been invoked. The coachman walked around to the door of his vehicle and spoke to someone within. John Culzean stood by and watched – and I waited in a puzzle.

Francis Bryan (2002), *Jim Hawkins and the Curse of Treasure Island*, Orion (pp. 7-8)

The old undertaker

My life started with a funeral, and might have ended there too, and no one any the wiser, or sadder, me included, if it hadn't been for Master Oakleigh, the old undertaker.

The called him that day to the workhouse in the town of —— in the West Country. A poor woman (rest her soul) had died in childbirth. The father (the devil will take care of him) was nowhere to be found. Her baby had died too, it seemed. And why not? Life was no bargain. So they called in Master Oakleigh to measure the body for the coffin. True it was only a poor woman and a plank box, but he was a craftsman and did his job with care.

So, when he found her lying there on an outhouse bench, her child clutched to her breast, he lifted the baby aside a moment to arrange her rags more decently.

And discovered, to his pleasure, not surprise for you cannot surprise an undertaker, that the child was not dead.

So, by chance my life had begun.

Robert Leeson (1985), *Silver's Revenge,* Collins (p. 11)

5 *Treasure Island*: Narration and point of view

Background

Treasure Island is narrated by Jim Hawkins. At the outset Jim explains that he has been asked to record the adventure by his companions. There are places in the narrative where we are reminded of the narrative context, where the narrator speaks directly to the reader. For example, 'I am not allowed to be more plain' (p. 87), and in Chapter 29 when Silver is presented with the black spot:

> The printed side had been blackened with wood ash, which already had begun to come off and soil my fingers; on the blank side had been written with the same material the one word "Depposed". I have that curiosity beside me at this moment; but not a trace of writing now remains beyond a single scratch, such as a man might make with his thumb-nail. (p. 253)

Although narrated in the first person, there are some passages where the persona of the narrator is less in evidence and comes closer to a third person perspective (e.g. pp. 165–7 Silver's parley with Captain Smollett).

The effect of this first person narrative is that the reader is only party to those plot developments that Jim witnesses. He describes his state of mind, feelings, and attitudes throughout the story, for example when he reflects on the impact that Billy Bones has on custom at the Admiral Benbow: 'My father was always saying the inn would be ruined, for people would soon cease coming there to be tyrannised over and put down, and sent shivering to their beds; but I really believe his presence did us good' (p. 7). Later, Jim demonstrates awareness of the implications of his actions: 'I was a fool, if you like, and certainly I was going to do a foolish, over bold act; but I was determined to do it with all the precautions in my power' (p. 185). For this reason, Dr Livesey narrates Chapters 16–18, when Jim is separated from his allies; this allows the story of how the ship was abandoned to be told. Livesey's narration is noticeably more formal than Jim's and he pays more attention to the unhealthy conditions of the island: 'if ever a man smelt fever and dysentery, it was in that abominable anchorage' (p. 135).

With regard to point of view, Chapter 28 is particularly interesting. Jim is captured and held in the pirates' stronghold. Stevenson invites the reader to view the mutineers from a different perspective. There is some suggestion that while human behaviour may be considered reprehensible from one perspective, it is acceptable from another.

National Curriculum reference to this type of work

The activities in this section focus on the identification of differences between the author, narrator and character (En2). Hot-seating the different characters will allow children to explore the story from different perspectives and is a supportive precursor to writing a narrative from a different point of view. The activity provides an opportunity for children to ask relevant questions, to clarify, extend and followup ideas as well as listening with attention in order to respond to others, taking account of what they say (En 1).

Specific NLS references

Year 5 Term 3 **T2** To identify the point of view from which a story is told and how this affects the reader's response.

Year 5 Term 3 **T3** To change point of view, e.g. tell incident or describe a situation from the point of view of another character or perspective.

Year 6 Term 1 **T2** To take account of viewpoint in a novel through
- identifying the narrator
- explaining how this influences the reader's view of events
- explaining how events might look from a different point of view.

Activity: Whose point of view?

Objective
- To change point of view, e.g. tell incident or describe a situation from the point of view of another character or perspective.
- To consider how Silver would describe the search and loss of Flint's treasure and to write about it from his point of view.

Outcome
Rewritten episode from Silver's point of view.

Resources
Copies of *Treasure Island*.

Teacher notes
When Silver and his followers are tricked out of the gold by Dr Livesey and Ben Gunn, Jim ends the Chapter:

> What a supper I had of it that night, with all my friends around me: and what a meal it was with Ben Gunn's salted goat, and some delicacies and a bottle of wine from the *Hispaniola*. Never, I am sure, were people gayer or happier. And there was Silver, sitting back almost out of the firelight, but eating heartily, prompt to spring forward when anything was wanted, even joining quietly in our laughter – the same bland, polite obsequious seaman of the voyage out. (p. 290)

Invite the children to suggest how Jim is feeling at this point of the story. Which words or phrases help to convey his feelings?

You might read or reread Chapter 34 and then consider what Silver might have been thinking during the feast. Why, for instance, might he be sitting back from the firelight or springing forward when anything was wanted? In what ways might Silver's perspective of the scene be different to Jim's? Encourage the children to back up their views with evidence from the text. Invite them to suggest questions they would like to ask Silver if he were to walk in the room.

Hot-seating is a good way to explore different perspectives, enabling the children to develop deeper understanding of the text. Arrange the seats in a circle. Ask if anyone would like to be Long John Silver. Invite the rest of the class to pose their questions. Pause to reflect on what they have discovered about the character. Ask if anyone has a different idea about Silver's thoughts and feelings. Invite a second child to take the hot-seat and repeat the activity. When the questioning is completed, pause to compare the similarities and differences with the first hot-seating session. By having more than one child in the hot-seat you are demonstrating that the activity is exploratory and that there may be more than one answer to a question. You can guide the children to consider whether both interpretations are equally plausible. You may want to put yourself in the hot-seat if, for instance, the children are not familiar with the technique or you want to challenge the children's thinking or problematise an issue.

Follow up this activity by asking the children to rewrite the scene from Long John Silver's perspective.

You could take this work further by extending it to the other characters and writing the scene from multiple perspectives. The children could read and record their writing onto audio-cassette to produce a resource for the listening area.

6 *Treasure Island*: Characters

Background

In *Treasure Island,* Stevenson created a gallery of memorable characters. Main characters and minor characters provide opportunities for studying character development, functions, moral ambiguity and humour.

Character and personal growth

Jim is the young narrator of most of the story, so the reader is party to his thoughts, feelings and perceptions. Jim is at the centre of the action: he discovers the treasure map, discovers Silver's plan, his encounter with Ben Gunn leads to the recovery of the treasure, and he provides the means of escape from the island by retaking the *Hispaniola*.

The character traits Jim displays include bravery, loyalty and an adventurous spirit. We learn about Jim through his actions and from the comments and reactions of other characters. His good qualities are recognised by both sides and even Silver admires him. Jim's father dies in the early Chapters of the book and a number of characters take on the role of surrogate father during the course of the story: Billy Bones at the Admiral Benbow inn, then Silver and Dr Livesey.

Jim's character develops during the course of the story and offers opportunities for children to look at character change and development. At the beginning he is a passive observer. The change is gradual, but the first indication is given in Chapter 4 when he takes control and helps his mother to safety. At the sign of The Spyglass in Bristol he is easily duped by Silver into believing that he has no connection with Black Dog or Billy Bones. He takes a rebellious dislike to Captain Smollett for no other reason than he has been told to work and the captain has said he will 'have no favourites'. His early actions serve to show his lack of dependability: 'I will confess that I was far too much taken up with what was going on to be of the slightest use as a sentry; indeed, I had already deserted my eastern loophole.' Later he starts to develop greater self awareness: 'I was a fool, if you like, and certainly I was going to do a foolish, over bold act, but I was determined to do it with all the precautions in my power' (p. 185). A key moment in Jim's development occurs when he overhears the mutineers' plans while hidden in the apple barrel. At this point he becomes aware of the duality of Silver's personality. In Chapter 28, we can see how far Jim has developed when he courageously stands up to the pirates: 'I no more fear you than I fear a fly.'

The final lines of the novel are an indication of the extent to which Jim has changed:

> The bar silver and the arms still lie, for all that I know, where Flint buried them; and certainly they shall lie there for me. Oxen and wain-ropes would not bring me back again to that accursed island; and the worst dreams that ever I have are when I hear the surf booming about its coasts, or start upright in bed, with the sharp voice of Captain Flint still ringing in my ears: 'Pieces of eight! pieces of eight!' (p. 298)

As a result of his adventure, Jim has realised that he does want the treasure, and that he is happy to leave the silver buried on the island. The negative tone that closes the story might be unexpected – after all everything has worked out for the best – but the last lines show that Jim remains troubled by the greed.

The 'good' characters

Squire Trelawney is a member of the landed gentry and is depicted as likeable but naïve and easily duped. He is self important, awarding himself the title 'admiral' though later he comes to accept the command of Captain Smollett: 'You were right and I was wrong. I own myself an ass, and I await your orders' (p. 103). Dr Livesey has the measure of the Squire from the outset when he states that he is the only man that he is afraid of as he cannot be trusted to be discreet. Trelawney proves to be a bad judge of character. He identifies Silver as 'a perfect trump' (p. 72) but dislikes the Captain for his forthright manner: 'that intolerable humbug, I declare I think his conduct unmanly, unsailorly, and downright unEnglish.'

Captain Smollett is the antithesis of the Squire. His judgements are proved to be sound: he is suspicious of the crew from the outset and fears that Mr Arrow will not make a good officer. He is forthright, 'better speak plain, I believe even at the risk of offence' (p. 74), and proves to be highly disciplined in his organisation of the defence of the stockade (Ch. 21). Children can fruitfully compare the presentation of Captain Smollett's character with the Squire's or with Silver's.

Dr Livesey is fair and intelligent and often takes on the role of arbitrator. His concern to do the right thing is evident from his treatment of Billy Bones; on the one hand he chastises Bones for causing upset at the inn, but also gives him medical treatment when he suffers a stroke. Livesey's actions show him to be caring: he provides medical treatment for the fever-stricken pirates and shows concern for those left behind on the island. He fails to get the measure of Silver's character early on, but perhaps he is responding intuitively to Silver's finer qualities: 'I don't put much faith in your discoveries, as a general thing; but I will say this, John Silver suits me' (p. 72). Livesey narrates Chapters 16–18. The narration of these Chapters is more formal and makes frequent mention of the malarial swamps.

A colourful cast of pirates

The pirates are grotesque characters, larger than life, outlandish and bizarre. Stevenson's exaggerated physical descriptions add a frisson of fear to the story. The equation of physical disability with unpleasantness has been criticised in recent years, but it is a fact that many pirates did have terrible injuries and missing limbs were common. Billy Bones' arrival at the Admiral Benbow immediately shatters the equilibrium:

> I remember him as if it were yesterday, as he came plodding to the inn door, his sea-chest following behind him in a hand-barrow; a tall, strong, heavy, nut-brown man; his tarry pigtail falling over the shoulders of his soiled blue coat; his hands ragged and scarred, with black broken nails; and the sabre cut across one cheek, a dirty livid white. (p. 3)

Although a fearsome character he is, in spite of his hot temper, kind to Jim, who willingly runs errands for him. Bones' relationship with Jim foreshadows the later relationship with Silver.

Black Dog's arrival at the Admiral Benbow starts the chain of violent events. Jim observes, 'He was a pale, tallowy creature, wanting two fingers of the left hand; and though he wore a cutlass, he did not look much like a fighter' (p. 13). When Black Dog fails to secure Flint's treasure map, Blind Pew arrives to issue the 'Black Spot'. He is the most terrifying of them all: 'He was plainly blind, for he tapped before him with a stick, and wore a great green shade over his eyes and nose; and he was hunched as if with age or weakness, and wore a huge old tattered sea-cloak with a hood, that made him appear positively deformed. I never saw in my life a more dreadful looking figure' (p. 26). Pew may be blind but he has an iron grip and instils terror in Jim and Bones.

The rogues' gallery is expanded with the hiring of the *Hispaniola*'s crew. Israel Hands, the coxswain, and previously Flint's gunner, is crafty and cunning. He shows no hesitation attempting to kill Jim.

Character and moral ambiguity

Stevenson's characterisation of Long John Silver is a masterpiece. He is the most vivid of the characters and the most complex, being neither good nor bad and displaying traits of both hero and villain. Some children may well respond with uncertainty or unease to Silver's character. On the positive side, Silver takes care of Jim and seems to have some genuine affection for the boy, but his actions also show that he is capable of cruel, murderous acts which he performs without remorse (p. 121). He is above all a pragmatist, taking the course of action that suits his purposes, to survive and win the treasure. He is surprisingly dexterous and in spite of his disability, physically strong. The descriptions of Silver given on Photocopiable sheets 6.2 to 6.4 (pp. 61–63) present different aspects of his character. Silver's dialogue is colourful and contains some memorable lines: 'Before an hour's out. I'll stove in your old blockhouse like a rum puncheon. Laugh by thunder, by thunder, laugh! Before the hour's out, ye'll laugh upon the other side. Them that die'll be the lucky ones' (p. 170).

Stevenson originally called his novel *The Sea Cook,* an indication of Silver's central importance in the novel. In his essay 'My First Book', Stevenson described where his inspiration for the character came from: 'I had an idea for John Silver from which I promised myself funds of entertainment; to take an admired friend of mine . . . to deprive him of all his finer qualities and higher graces of temperament, to leave him with nothing but his strength, his courage, his quickness, and his magnificent geniality.'

Character and humorous interlude

Ben Gunn provides light comic relief. He first appears after Silver shockingly kills the honest sailor, Tom. Marooned on the island for three years, Jim cannot at first tell whether he is man or beast. Gunn's description owes a lot to his literary antecedent, Robinson Crusoe:

> I could see now that he was a white man like myself, and that his features were even pleasing. His skin, wherever it was exposed, was burnt by the sun; even his lips were black; and his fair eyes looked quite startling in so dark a face. Of all the beggar-men that I had seen or fancied, he was the chief for raggedness. He was clothed with tatters of old ship's canvas and old sea cloth; and this extraordinary patchwork was held together by a system of the most various and incongruous fastenings, brass buttons, bits of stick, and loops of tarry gaskin. About his waist he wore an old brass-buckled leather belt, which was the one thing solid in his whole accoutrement. (p. 126)

Stevenson makes use of the popular device of having his comic character mispronounce words (e.g. 'chapling' for 'chaplin'). Gunn dreams of toasted cheese and is dismissed as mad, but he holds the key to finding the treasure.

National Curriculum reference to this type of work

The National Curriculum requires that children are given opportunities to participate in a wide range of drama activities, including the use of dramatic techniques to explore characters (En1). Children can use drama as a means of exploring the moral question: 'Should Jim Hawkins trust long John Silver?' The character activities outlined in this section require pupils to engage in reading which is beyond the literal; they will, for instance, be able to consider character motivations and alternative perspectives (En2). The curriculum also states that pupils should be taught how language varies between standard and dialect forms. Stevenson's skilful use of dialogue to develop character provides a good opportunity to investigate standard and non-standard uses of language (En1).

Specific NLS references

Year 4 Term 1	T1	To investigate how settings and characters are built up from small details, and how the reader responds to them.
Year 4 Term 1	T2	To identify the main characteristics of the key characters, drawing on the text to justify views and using the information to predict actions.
Year 4 Term 3	T1	To identify social, moral or cultural issues in stories, e.g. the dilemmas faced by characters, and to discuss how the characters deal with them; to locate evidence in the text.
Year 5 Term 1	T3	To investigate how characters are presented, referring to the text: • through dialogue, action and description • how the reader responds to them (as victims, heroes, etc.) • through examining their relationships with other characters.

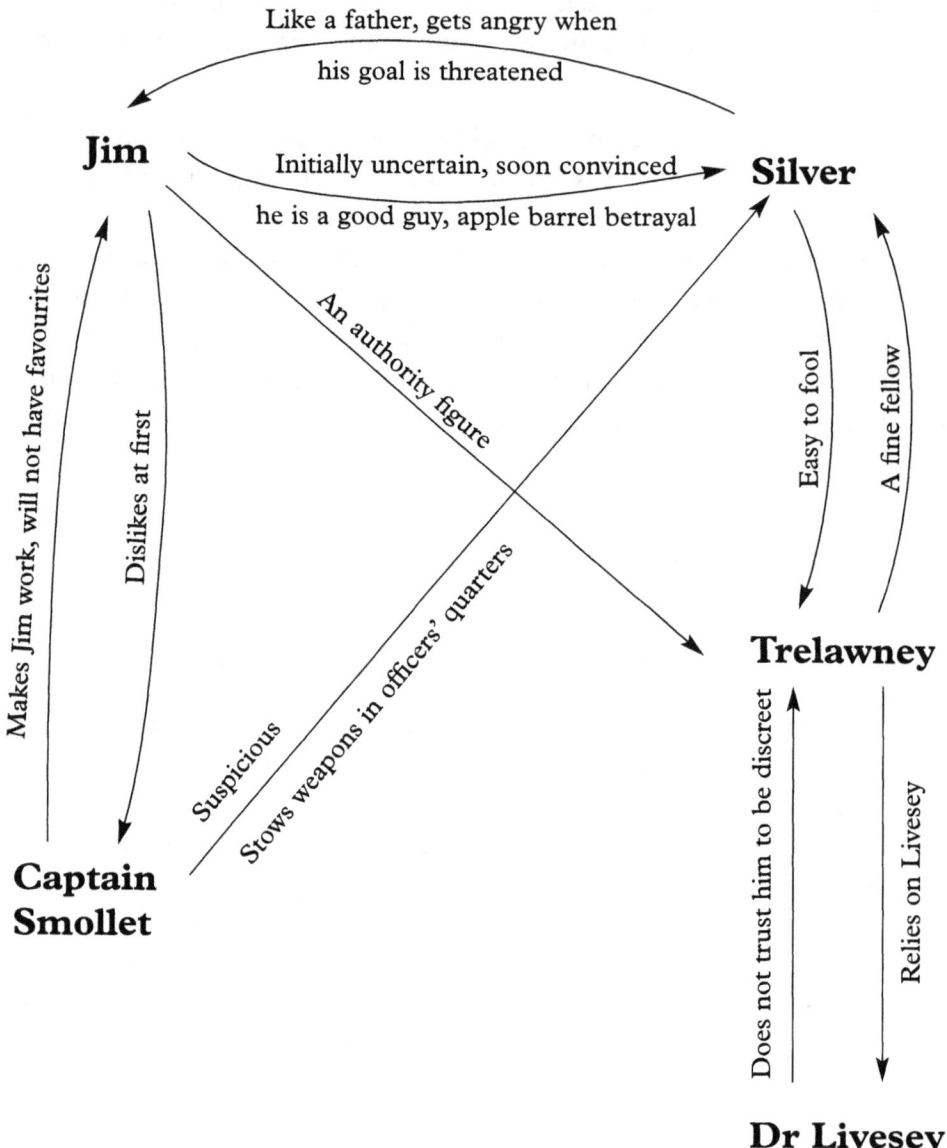

Partially completed sociogram showing characters' relationships. The diagram can be added to as the characters' opinions change, and key quotations can be included.

Activity: Long John Silver – hero or villain?

Objective
- To look at ways in which characters are developed.
- To investigate affective responses to character.

Outcome
Debate: 'Is Long John Silver a hero or a villain?'

Resources
Large sheet of paper and marker pens; copies of extracts; copies of *Treasure Island*.

Teacher notes
The following is a suggested order for activities exploring Long John Silver's character. The 'role on the wall' activity allows open exploration, and responses are likely to be more varied than if starting with the text analysis. Implicitly held opinions can be examined and supporting evidence discussed. The strategy encourages children to draw on their own experiences and feelings.

The 'role on the wall' technique can be used to stimulate a discussion about different perceptions of Long John Silver's character. On a large sheet of paper, draw an outline of the character. In pairs or small groups, ask the children to write with marker pens on strips of paper or card: what they *know* about Silver; what they *think* they know about him; and what they *feel* about him. Then ask them to attach their pieces of paper to the outline. When all the ideas have been attached read them aloud with the class. Discuss which ideas crop up most frequently. Are there any conflicting opinions? Why might this be the case? Encourage the children to refer to evidence in the text to support their views.

(Note: you might use the same technique as an opening for looking at other characters or comparing characters. For example, comparing Long John Silver with Doctor Livesey or Squire Trelawney with Captain Smollett.)

Following the 'role on the wall' activity, you might ask the children to propose questions that they would like to ask Silver and then ask for volunteers to be hot-seated (see Introduction).

Text analysis: a closer look at the evidence
Prepare copies of the descriptions of Silver on Photocopiable sheets 6.2 to 6.4. Read the first passage. In pairs, ask the children to highlight any words and phrases that describe Silver. Draw attention to the similes, 'hopping about upon it like a bird', 'a face as big as a ham', and discuss their effect. Highlight the adjectives and verbs in different colours (e.g. adjectives: 'merry', 'cheerful', 'clean', 'pleasant'; verbs: 'whistling', 'smiling'). Consider whether the vocabulary choice helps to build a positive, neutral or negative image of Silver.

Read the second or third passage and follow the same procedure. Compare the images of Long John Silver, including the different animals that he is compared to. Discuss whether it is authentic for a character to have more than one side to their personality. Draw on children's experiences, asking them to think about their own most positive traits and less favourable ones.

Ask the children to suggest events where Silver shows a positive side to his character and make a list including page references. Do the same for incidents where Silver displays negative character traits.

Positive character traits	Negative character traits

The debate: Is Long John Silver a hero or villain?
Independently or in pairs, ask half the children to write a case for Silver and half to write the case against. Ask them to consider, in addition to the above question, whether Jim was right to trust Silver. Explain that they will be presenting their evidence at a trial so they will need to be as persuasive as possible. You might review different features of writing argument before the children construct their arguments.

Divide the class into three groups, one third to present in favour of Silver, one third against and one third to be the jury (who will listen to both sides of the argument and cast a vote at the end of the trial). Ask for a volunteer to read their argument to open the case for Silver. Invite those opposing to ask questions of those in favour. Repeat the process with the case against. Ask for two volunteers to sum up the arguments. Finally, ask the jury to vote in favour or against by placing either a blank piece of paper (for) or one marked with a black spot (against) into a ballot box.

Activity: Character development and change

Objective
To consider how Jim changes throughout the novel using evidence from text.

Outcome
Graphic representation of character change and development.

Resources
Copies of Photocopiable sheet 6.1 'Character scale'; copies of *Treasure Island* or selected extracts.

Teacher notes
One of the major themes of *Treasure Island* is the development from dependence to autonomy of the main character, Jim Hawkins.

Locate and read a passage from an early part of the novel in which Jim's role is essentially passive, e.g. his reaction to Billy Bones. Ask the children to suggest words to describe Jim. Select and read another key moment towards the end of the novel and repeat the process. You could chart the differences in character graphically using a set of scales, e.g. timid → courageous, responsible → irresponsible, dependent → independent, helpful → unhelpful, selfish → selfless, etc.

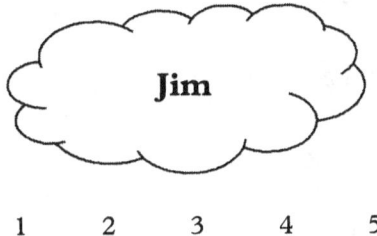

1   2   3   4   5

Timid	Courageous
Responsible	Irresponsible
Dependent	Independent
Selfish	Selfless
Clueless	Resourceful
Foolish	Sensible
Sad	Happy

Use different pairs of words and complete at different stages thrroughout study of the novel.

Construct a sociogram showing Jim's relationship with each of the characters. What does Jim think about them? What do they think about Jim? You might want to add some key quotations to your chart.

Activity: Character through dialogue

Objective
To look at the way in which character can be presented through dialogue.

Outcome
Scripted dialogue.

Resources
Copies of the Photocopiable sheet 6.2 to 6.4 (alternatively, use different extracts which show character through dialogue, for example Silver's parley with Captain Smollett); highlighter pens.

Teacher notes
Stevenson presents some lively dialogue, using pace, rhythm and colourful vocabulary, in which you can almost hear the characters speaking off the page. A particularly fine example is the argument between Silver and the rest of the pirates when they tip him the black spot (Photocopiable sheet 6.4).

Read the extract aloud and briefly discuss the different characters that emerge in this episode, drawing attention to Stevenson's vocabulary choices and patterns of language. Discuss personal reactions to the characters. Discuss the use of non-Standard English. You might want to verbally transpose the dialogue into Standard English to hear how the dialogue influences the reader's image of the characters. Highlight the direct speech, recapping the way direct speech is presented and punctuated. Ask the children to practise reading the dialogue in groups of four and then ask volunteer groups to read the passage. Listening to the same passage read by different voices will draw out different aspects of personality. Ask them to comment on what they like about each other's reading and give praise for drawing out the contrasting personalities of the pirates.

As a shared writing activity, show how the dialogue can be transposed into scripted dialogue, drawing attention to the conventions of layout and punctuation. You can extend this work by asking the children to invent a different scenario with the pirates and to improvise a short scene which can then be scripted. To help them get started you could prepare a set of possible scenario cards and ask each group to select one, e.g. the pirates discover that the *Hispaniola* has disappeared. You might also look at the way other characters are presented through dialogue, as the Squire, the Captain and Doctor Livesey have distinctive ways of speaking.

Long John Silver: Description 1

As I was waiting, a man came out of a side room, and, at a glance, I was sure he must be Long John. His left leg was cut off close by the hip, and under the left shoulder he carried a crutch, which he managed with wonderful dexterity, hopping about upon it like a bird. He was very tall and strong, with a face as big as a ham – plain and pale, but intelligent and smiling. Indeed he seemed in the most cheerful spirits, whistling as he moved about among the tables, with a merry word or a slap on the shoulder for the more favoured of his guests.

Now to tell the truth, from the very first mention of Long John in Squire Trelawney's letter, I had taken a fear in my mind that he might prove to be the very one-legged sailor whom I had watched for so long at the old 'Benbow'. But one look at the man before me was enough. I had seen the captain, and Black Dog, and the blind man Pew, and I thought I knew what a buccaneer was like – a very different creature according to me, from this clean and pleasant tempered landlord.

Treasure Island, pp. 63–5

Long John Silver: Description 2

'He's no common man, Barbecue,' said the coxswain to me. 'He had good schooling in his young days, and can speak like a book when so minded; and brave – a lion's nothing alongside of Long John! I've seen him grapple four, and knock their heads together – him unarmed.'

All the crew respected and even obeyed him. He had a way of talking to each, and doing everybody some particular service. To me he was unweariedly kind; and always glad to see me in the galley, which he kept as clean as a new pin; the dishes hanging up burnished, and his parrot in a cage in one corner.

Treasure Island, p. 84

Long John Silver: Description 3

And with that this brave fellow turned his back directly on the cook, and set off walking for the beach. But he was not destined to go far. With a cry, John seized the branch of a tree, whipped the crutch out of his arm-pit, and sent that uncouth missile hurtling through the air. It struck poor Tom, point foremost, and with stunning violence, right between his shoulders in the middle of his back. His hands flew up, he gave a sort of gasp, and fell.

Whether he were injured much or little, none could ever tell. Like enough, to judge from the sound, his back was broken on the spot. But he had no time given him to recover. Silver, agile as a monkey, even without leg or crutch, was on top of him next moment, and had twice buried his knife up to the hilt in that defenceless body. From my place of ambush, I could hear him pant aloud as he struck the blows.

Treasure Island, p. 62

The black spot again

The sea cook looked at what had been given him.

'The black spot! I thought so,' he observed.

'Where might you have got the paper? Why, hillo! Look here, now: this ain't lucky! You've gone and cut this out of a Bible. What fool's cut a Bible?'

'Ha, there!' said Morgan – 'There! Wot did I say? No good'll come o' that, I said.'

'Well, you've fixed it now, among you,' continued Silver. 'You'll swing now, I reckon. What soft-hearted lubber had a Bible?'

'It was Dick,' said one.

'Dick, was it? Then Dick can get to prayers,' said Silver. 'He's seen his slice of luck, has Dick, and you may lay to that.'

But here the long man with the yellow eyes struck in.

'Belay that talk, John Silver,' he said. 'This crew has tipped you the black spot in full council, as in dooty bound; just turn it over, as in dooty bound, and see what's wrote there. Then you can talk.'

'Thanky, George,' replied the sea cook. 'You always was brisk for business, and has the rules by heart, George, as I'm pleased to see. Well, what is it anyway? Ah! "Deposed" – that's it, is it? Very pretty wrote, to be sure; like print, I swear. Your hand o' write George? Why you was gettin' quite a leadin' man in this here crew. You'll be cap'n next, I shouldn't wonder.'

Treasure Island, pp. 247–8

7 *Treasure Island*: Setting

Background

Treasure Island is set in three places: the Admiral Benbow, aboard the *Hispaniola* and Treasure Island.

The Admiral Benbow, described as a lonely inn set in a cove on a rugged west country coastline, is run by Jim's Hawkins' parents. Billy Bones chooses to reside at the inn because it has few visitors and there is a good vantage point close by to watch for ships.

The second part of the story takes place on board a schooner, the *Hispaniola*. The ship is described in accurate detail in Chapter 10. The children can take part in context-building exercises, such as researching ships of the period and investigating the definitions of topic vocabulary relating to ships and shipping (see poster challenge). The ship also serves a symbolic function in the story, representing the transition from civilisation to the savagery of the island.

When they reach the island a sense of reality sets in. It is not what Jim had imagined and is probably not the picture of a treasure island that most of the children will have. Jim describes his first impressions:

> Grey-coloured woods covered a large part of the surface. This even tint was indeed broken up by streaks of yellow sandbank in the lower lands, and by many tall trees of the pine family, out-topping the others – some singly, some in clumps; but the general colouring was uniform and sad. (p. 109)

Later, he notices 'two swamps, emptied out into this pond . . . And the foliage round that part of the shore had a kind of poisonous brightness.' Livesey also emphasises negative aspects of the island: 'the nasty stench of the place turned me sick, if ever a man smelt fear and dysentery, it was in that abominable anchorage' (p. 135). Treasure Island, also aptly named Skeleton Island, is no paradise. Key descriptions of the island are found in Chapters 12–16. And in Chapter 20 we are reminded of the direct impact that the setting has on the plot. It is the pirates' poor choice of camp that leads to illness and Silver's inability to cope with the hilly sandy terrain and his consequent humiliation that prompts him to lead the fierce attack on the stockade. Stevenson's descriptions of the island are a great starting point for creative exploration in drama, music and art.

National Curriculum reference to this type of work

The National Curriculum emphasises the importance of developing an appreciation of literary texts, including the choice, use and effect of figurative language, vocabulary and patterns of language. This objective can be addressed by activities that aim to refine children's responses to Stevenson's creation of the island setting, such as set designing/building. Children's imaginative responses can also be developed through the creation of sound collages to reflect the moods that are evoked by the writing (En 2).

Specific NLS references

Year 4 Term 1	**T1**	To investigate how settings are built up from small details and how the reader responds to them.
Year 4 Term 2	**T2**	To understand how settings influence events and incidents in stories and how they affect characters' behaviour.
Year 4 Term 2	**T4**	To understand how the use of expressive and descriptive language can, e.g., create moods, arouse expectations, build tension.
Year 6 Term 1	**T9**	To prepare a short section of a story as a script, using location/setting.

Activity: Designing a film set

Objectives
To analyse an extract which describes the island setting in order to design a film set.

Outcome
Design a film or stage set for *Treasure Island*.

Resources
Copies of Photocopiable sheet 7.1; page references for alternative passages that describe different parts of *Treasure Island*; highlighter pens; an enlarged copy of the map of *Treasure Island*; large sheets of paper for collaborative drawing; copies of *Treasure Island*.

Teacher notes
Start by analysing the passage with the class. Read it aloud and then ask the children to work in pairs to talk about their initial impressions. Does the description match their ideas of what a treasure island looks like? Ask them to highlight words and phrases that help build a sense of place. Next, ask them to highlight words or phrases that indicate how Jim is feeling with a different colour.

You might prompt the children to imagine themselves on the island: what would it be like? what would you do? One way of doing this is to use the 'eye-in-the sky' visualisation technique. Invite pupils to close their eyes if they find it helps them to see images more clearly. Then talk them through the scene: 'Imagine you are looking down on the island from a point high in the sky. What does it look like? You move in closer. Now you can see the tops of the trees. Do you notice anything moving in the trees? What do the trees look like? What colours do you notice? Now you are moving closer through the branches of the trees. What can you hear close by and in the distance?' Gradually zoom in until they are imagining themselves standing on the ground and able to move around and pick things up.

In pairs or small groups the children can design film or stage sets for different parts of the island. The talk that accompanies collaborative drawing provides opportunities for children to develop a shared understanding and can aid the development of response.

Decide how many different scenes you would need (e.g. Silver's camp, the stockade area, the inner island where Jim finds Ben Gunn, etc). Different groups can design a set for a different part of the island. Help the groups to find the relevant references to the setting in the text and provide them with large sheets of paper and drawing materials. In designing the set they should pay attention to:

- layout
- colour (paint charts can be cut up and used to make colour sections or to select a colour scheme)
- objects/props
- design notes can be added to provide extra information if needed, for example the sounds that can be heard.

Share and evaluate designs. Consider how effectively the designs convey the mood and atmosphere of the island as described by Stevenson.

Make a display with the Treasure Map at the centre showing where the different sets are located. The activity could be extended with children building models of the sets as part of a design technology project.

Activity: Sound collage

Objectives
- To respond creatively to Stevenson's descriptions of setting.
- To understand how expressive and descriptive language can create moods.

Outcome
A sound collage to capture the mood of the sea or the island as described by Stevenson.

Resources
Copies of Photocopiable sheet 7.1; a range of percussion instruments.

Teacher notes
Select a passage which describes an aspect of setting, e.g. a description of the island or the sea voyage. Read it aloud and then ask the children to work in pairs to talk about their initial impressions.

To create the sound collage, you can either work entirely with voices or use a combination of voices, body noises (e.g. foot tapping) and percussion instruments. Form a circle. Ask each child in turn to suggest a sound that reflects the atmosphere of the setting. Each child must suggest a different sound. Sounds can include words from the passage, e.g. 'Spy-glass trembled through the haze'. Encourage the children to use appropriate vocal tones and instruments if you are using them. When you have heard all of the sounds individually, briefly consider whether they are all suited to the mood you are trying to create. If necessary select some new sounds. You will need to remember where the different sounds are in the circle. You might want to group sounds together (e.g. animal noises), but it can also be effective to have them distributed around the circle. Agree some signals with the children that will help you to conduct your sound collage, e.g. start, stop, louder, softer, faster, slower, etc. Now you are ready to start conducting – start with the sounds that will make a good introduction. After you have performed the piece, ask the children to evaluate it. It can be quite useful to have a few observers who do not participate but instead give feedback on the effect created and suggest improvements. Have another go, inviting volunteers to take over the role of 'conductor'.

When you are happy with your sound collage you might want to find a way of recording it so that the performance can be repeated. The sound collage can be used as an introduction to reading a passage or Chapter, or alternatively you might want to combine it with the theme park tableaux activity (p. 38).

The island setting

I was so pleased at having given the slip to Long John, that I began to enjoy myself and look around me with some interest on the strange land that I was in.

I had crossed a marshy tract full of willows, bulrushes, and odd, outlandish, swampy trees; and I had now come out upon the skirts of an open piece of undulating, sandy country, about a mile long, dotted with a few pines, and a great number of contorted trees, not unlike the oak in growth, but pale in the foliage, like willows. On the far side of the open stood one of the hills, with two quaint, craggy peaks, shining vividly in the sun.

I now felt for the first time the joy of exploration. The isle was uninhabited; my shipmates I had left behind, and nothing lived in front of me but dumb brutes and fowls. I turned hither and thither among the trees. Here and there were flowering plants, unknown to me; here and there I saw snakes, and one raised his head from a ledge of rock and hissed at me with a noise not unlike the spinning of a top. Little did I suppose that he was a deadly enemy, and that the noise was the famous rattle.

Then I came to a long thicket of these oak-like trees – live or evergreen oaks, I heard afterwards they should be called – which grew low along the sand like brambles, the boughs curiously twisted, the foliage compact, like thatch. The thicket stretched down from the top of one of the sandy knolls, spreading and growing taller as it went, until it reached the margin of the broad, reedy fen, through which the nearest of the little rivers soaked its way into the anchorage. The marsh was steaming in the strong sun, and the outline of the Spy-glass trembled through the haze.

Treasure Island, pp. 116–17

8   *Treasure Island*: Themes

Background

Themes in literature can be distinguished from the subject or content. The themes, or messages, are often implicit and not necessarily overtly stated. Different readers will respond to and identify with different themes within a novel, and as themes are at the heart of the way in which readers attribute meaning to what they read, it is important that space is allowed for individual response and interpretation. Responses will be determined by experiences and thematic relevance to readers. Some of the major themes that emerge in *Treasure Island* include friendship, trust, loyalty, the quest, good and evil, personal growth and maturation, fortune and luck. Children may well identify further themes.

The quest

The quest has been a recurring theme in literature since mythological times and involves a hero setting out on a voyage or journey to obtain a prize. In order to achieve their goal the hero has to overcome a series of obstacles or challenges. Examples include the search for the Holy Grail in Arthurian legend, and the quest for the Golden Fleece in Greek mythology. In contrast with these 'worthy' quest tales, the goal in *Treasure Island*, Flint's treasure, is of questionable worth (it is stolen) and the quest is motivated primarily through greed. Throughout the story the reader is constantly reminded that the treasure is the ultimate goal. Even when the characters are in perilous circumstances, finding treasure is seen to be more important than survival (Chapter 20).

If *Treasure Island* is a romantic quest, then Jim Hawkins is the hero. The quest hero usually learns equally from the successes and failures that are experienced during the journey. Traditionally, the heroes of quest literature have been male, but there are some good examples of female heroes, for example Lyra in Philip Pullman's *His Dark Materials* trilogy, Ronia in Astrid Lindgren's *Ronia, the Robber's Daughter,* Dorothy in Frank L. Baum's *The Wizard of Oz*, Garth Nix's *Sabriel* and Lara Croft in *Tomb Raider*. Quests will often feature maps like Flint's treasure map (e.g. in *Watership Down*, *The Lord of the Rings* and *Lara Croft: the Cradle of Life*). Imaginative map-making can help children find ideas for writing their own quest stories or for developing drama. Many children will be familiar with the idea of the quest, not only from traditional tales but from popular culture, including game shows, computer games and film. They can be encouraged to make connections and to compare how the quest theme is handled in *Treasure Island* and other known texts.

Personal growth

One of the major recurring themes in *Treasure Island* is the growth to maturity of the narrator Jim Hawkins. At the outset Jim is passive, as is evidenced in the way he is ordered about by Billy Bones and Blind Pew. With the death of Bones, Jim begins to exert some control, for example he is able to guide his mother to safety and makes the decision to take the treasure map to Dr Livesey despite personal risk. Further evidence of personal development can be seen in Chapter 21 (the way in which he contributes to the defence of the stockade) and Chapter 22 (his rationalisation of the course of action he chooses). He also makes a moral decision to keep his promise to Silver rather than escaping when Dr Livesey urges him to (see p. 58 for an activity about character and personal growth).

Good and evil

On the surface, *Treasure Island* may seem to be concerned with a battle between the 'goodies' and 'baddies'. The story is set up so that the reader is led to think in terms of 'our side' and 'the others'. In Chapter 11, after hearing the mutineers' plans, Jim reflects on his concern for all the 'honest' men aboard the ship. But both sides are seeking the treasure and are willing to use similar tactics – and the whole expedition has been motivated by greed. So the reader does not choose sides on the basis of the moral superiority of one group over another. However, the 'good' characters are depicted with more positive characteristics: they display courage, organisation and discipline, whereas the pirates are cowardly and lack discipline (see, for example, Chapter 21).

The moral ambiguity of *Treasure Island* is most evident in the dual personality of Long John Silver. At the outset Silver is held in good opinion by everyone except Captain Smollett. Even Israel Hands talks about him with warmth and respect. Silver befriends Jim and adopts the role of surrogate father. One of the novel's most crucial moments reveals the lengths to which Silver is willing to go to win the treasure: when he murders Tom, an innocent and honest seaman, in cold blood.

National Curriculum reference to this type of work

The National Curriculum states that children should be taught to identify how themes are developed and to evaluate ideas and themes that broaden perspectives. The theme or themes in books are not necessarily overtly stated, so exploration and engagement with the thematic content will inevitably provide opportunities for children to develop skills in reading beyond the literal (En2).

Specific NLS objectives

Year 4 Term 2	**T2**		To review a range of stories, identifying themes or treatments.
Year 4 Term 3	**T8**		To write critically about an issue or dilemma raised in a story, explaining the problem, alternative courses of action and evaluating the writer's solution.
Year 6 Term 2	**T7**		To identify the key features of different types of literary text, e.g. stock characters, plot structure and how particular texts conform, develop or undermine the type.
Year 6 Term 3	**T6**		To look at connections and contrasts in the work of different writers.

Activity: The quest

Objectives
- To identify the characteristic features of quest stories.
- To evaluate *Treasure Island* as a quest story.
- To compare *Treasure Island* to other quest stories taking account of similarities and differences.
- To consider what might be learnt from quest stories.

Outcome
Class discussion.

Resources
Comics, computer games; film magazines; traditional stories with quest themes; copies of Photocopiable sheet 8.1.

Teacher notes
Look up different definitions of 'quest' in several dictionaries. Write the definitions on large sheets of paper or card and display them. Comparing definitions shows the children that dictionaries do not contain absolute meanings. Discuss which meanings of the word can be applied to *Treasure Island*.

Discuss the characteristics of a quest story and make a list of the children's suggestions. Consider the nature of the quest in *Treasure Island*. In pairs, ask children to complete the first column of Photocopiable sheet 8.1. Leave space to add questions suggested by the children (e.g. what kind of journey is undertaken).

Work in fours to share ideas and discuss any differences. The children may find some questions more difficult than others. For example in discussing whose quest it is, they may find it hard to choose between Jim, Squire Trelawney and Long John Silver.

Ask the children whether they know any other stories with quests. Encourage them to think of a range of texts including traditional stories, computer games and films. Ask them to select two quest texts that they know well and complete the table. What similarities or differences do they notice between them? More experienced readers can be encouraged to look at instances where type (such as the romantic hero) is undermined, and to identify parodies of the quest story.

Have a discussion about whether readers can learn anything from quest stories. Ask every child to jot down one idea about something that can be learned from a quest story and then ask them to read out their ideas in turn without commenting on their suggestions. This ensures that everyone has the opportunity to express their thoughts and that all ideas are treated as equally valid. Then ask the children if they found any of the ideas that were suggested particularly interesting. Use these ideas as a starting point for the discussion.

PHOTOCOPIABLE SHEET 8.1

The quest story

	Text 1 Treasure Island	Text 2	Text 3
What is the quest?			
What is the purpose or goal of the quest?			
Whose quest is it?			
Is the questor male or female?			
Is it a worthy or unworthy quest?			
What challenges or obstacles must be overcome on the journey?			
What failures are experienced?			
What successes are experienced?			
What is the outcome?			

9 Adaptations

Background

Treasure Island has inspired many adaptations, including no fewer than three Disney films (see resource list p. 91). Studying a film adaptation alongside the original text provides opportunities for children to work with a medium which is familiar to them. They will already have a wealth of knowledge and experience about the way in which films work, which will help them to make implicit knowledge explicit. Discussion of issues such as reading/viewing preferences, exploration of the choices made in the process of adaptation, representations and consideration of intended audience, etc. will support the development of critical literacy.

National Curriculum reference to this type of work

Looking at film adaptations of classic books provides an opportunity for children to discuss ideas through, for instance, evaluating the interpretation of a character in a film version, or planning a storyboard of a scene for their own adaptation (En1). The activities outlined below require children to look for meaning beyond the literal, to make connections between different parts of a text and to use knowledge of other texts they have read. Note: although only explicitly mentioned by the NLS in Year 6 Term 1, many of the text objectives can be addressed through film study.

Specific NLS objectives

Year 4 Term 1	**T1**	To investigate how settings and characters are built up from small details and how the reader (viewer) responds to them.
Year 4 Term 2	**T9**	To recognise how certain types of texts are targeted at particular readers (audiences).
Year 5 Term 1	**T1**	To analyse the features of a good opening and compare a number of story openings.
Year 5 Term 1	**T3**	To investigate how characters are presented, referring to the text: • through dialogue, action and description • how the reader responds to them (as victims, heroes, etc.) • through examining their relationships with other characters.
Year 6 Term 1	**T1**	To compare and evaluate a novel or play in print and the film/TV version, e.g. treatment of the plot and characters, the differences in the two forms, e.g. in seeing the setting, in losing the narrator.

Activity: Character and film

Objective
- To compare and evaluate a novel in print and film versions.
- To investigate how characters are presented in written and visual texts.
- To consider how the reader/viewer is invited to respond to them.

Outcome
Comparison of the representation of a character in the book and a film version.

Resources
Paper and drawing materials; copies of Photocopiable sheet 9.1 'Character adaptation'; one or more film versions of *Treasure Island*.

Teacher notes
One point for comparison is the way in which the adaptations deal with characterisation. The different interpretations of Long John Silver are particularly interesting and can be compared with each other as well as Stevenson's text. They range from the 'over the top' performance by Robert Newton in 1950 to a more understated performance by Charlton Heston in the 1990 Warner Brothers film; Tim Curry plays the one-legged pirate in *Muppet Treasure Island* (1996) and in Disney's *Treasure Planet* (2003), Silver is depicted as a cyborg.

Following a discussion about Stevenson's presentation of Silver (see p. 57), the children can be invited to make a labelled drawing to illustrate the way they would present him in a film version. Guide them to give some attention to expressions, gestures, posture, mannerisms and voice qualities, as well as general appearance including clothing and hairstyle. Use Photocopiable sheet 9.1 to aid comparison. You might ask the children which actor they would cast in the role if they were the casting director.

Compare their ideas with one or more of the film versions. You might select a key scene for comparison (e.g. the introduction of Silver at the Spyglass Inn, the parley with Dr Livesey, or the episode when Silver is given the black spot). What decisions have been taken about the way the character is presented? Is there anything they find surprising or interesting about the choices made? Are there things that can be in a film that cannot be presented in a book? Are there some things that are explored in the book that cannot be shown in the film? To what extent is the moral ambiguity of Stevenson's portrayal of Silver realised in the film versions?

The portrayal of the other characters can be analysed in a similar way.

Character adaptation

Character	Book	Film
General description		
Body language		
Clothing		
Speech and voice qualities		
Dialogue		
Way in which the reader/viewer is invited to respond to the character		

Activity: Investigating opening sequences

Objective
- To compare and evaluate a novel in print and film versions.
- To analyse the features of a good opening and compare several story openings.
- To recognise how certain types of text are targeted at particular readers.

Outcome
Comparison and evaluation of the film opening sequences with the novel opening and own storyboards.

Resources
Copies of *Treasure Island* or photocopies of the first chapter; different film versions of *Treasure Island*; blank storyboards.

Teacher notes
The way in which a film begins is crucial for gaining the audience interest and attention. Each of the film adaptations takes a very different approach, giving clues about genre and intended audience. For example, *Muppet Treasure Island* commences with a scene that is only implied in the book, Flint's burial of the treasure. The 1990 film starts with Billy Bones approaching a west country cove in his search for an isolated inn. *Treasure Planet* begins with a 15-year-old Jim Hawkins speeding around the port of Benbow on a makeshift solar surfer.

Drawing on the children's experiences, start by discussing how different films begin. For instance, some films such as James Bond start with a pre-titles action scene.

Reread the first chapter of *Treasure Island*. In pairs, ask the children to think about what they would include in their title sequence. They can then storyboard the sequence, which should be timed to last about four minutes. Tell them that they should make suggestions about the music or sound they would like to accompany the visuals, but should avoid the inclusion of dialogue.

Ask pairs to work in groups of four to present, compare and evaluate their ideas. With the whole class, invite children to discuss that they liked about each other's work.

View the opening of one of the film adaptations. Ask the children for first responses. What did they like/dislike? Were there any surprises? Were there any changes or additions not in the book? What mood was created by the choice of music? Invite them to consider why the production team may have decided to open the film in this way. Does the opening sequence give any clues about the intended audience? Now view and compare the opening sequences of other versions.

10 Three-week plan

Three-week plan

It is recommended that *Treasure Island* is read aloud to the class prior to starting work on this body of work. Week 3 focuses on the narrative structure, so the children will need a good grasp of the plot before they are able to carry out the activities suggested.

Week 1

Text level objectives

- To investigate how characters are presented and developed in *Treasure Island*.

Resources

- Selected passages focusing on character.
- Highlighter pens.
- Writing frame for composing argument, if needed.

Week 2

Text level objectives

- To investigate the film adaptation of a classic.
- To consider reasons for different ways of presenting scenes in visual and written texts.
- To develop an understanding of audience and the way in which an intended audience impacts on the choices made about presentation.

Resources

- Passages of key scenes, e.g. the opening.
- At least two video adaptations of *Treasure Island*.

Week 3

Text level objectives

- To analyse the features of a good opening.
- To explore narrative structure and the order of events.

Resources

- Copies of *Treasure Island*.
- Copies of sequels, e.g. Robert Leeson *Silver's Revenge* or photocopies of opening extracts (Photocopiable sheets 4.4 and 4.5).
- Photocopies of the opening of *Treasure Island* (Photocopiable sheet 4.3)
- Copies of Photocopiable sheet 4.1.

A large space for the run through of the tableaux will enhance the performance aspect of the work, but it is possible to run each scene in sequence in a classroom.

Three-week Plan

WEEK 1	Shared text work	Group	Independent	Plenary
Monday	Long John Silver: first thoughts. Role on the wall and discussion, e.g. what would the children like to know about Silver.	Character comparisons. Compare Long John Silver with one other character. Make a list of similarities and differences. Place each character on a range of numbered scales (from 1 to 5), e.g. honest – dishonest, clever – stupid.	Paired work: identify and write questions for hot-seating Silver. Select a challenge from the poster.	Hot-seat at least two children as Long John Silver. Encourage the children to reflect on what they have learnt from the hot-seating and relate this to the text.
Tuesday	Close reading. Read and annotate Photocopiable sheet 6.2. Suggest words that describe Silver's character and suggest synonyms.	Character comparisons (as above).	Paired work: compare sheet 6.2 with a contrasting passage on Silver. Highlight positive aspects of character with one colour and negative with another. Select a challenge from the poster.	Summarise positive and negative features. Consider how Stevenson's choice of vocabulary and use of language influence the reader's response. Review role on the wall activity. Have views have been confirmed or challenged?
Wednesday	Reread sheet 6.2 and consider the use of the animal simile. Discuss other examples of animal imagery used to describe the pirates. Create some positive and negative images using animal imagery.	Character comparisons (as above).	Paired work: Make a bulleted list of either the negative or positive aspects of Silver's character. Make a picture of Silver using the list and the evidence identified in the text.	Share ideas. Add new suggestions to lists as appropriate. Display the pictures. Praise use of evidence from the text to emphasise characteristics.

WEEK 1	Shared text work	Group	Independent	Plenary	
Thursday	Read and annotate a passage which reveals Silver's character through dialogue. Consider vocabulary choices, manner of speech, etc.	Character comparisons (as above).	Should Jim trust Long John Silver? Prepare a case for or against. In small groups, construct a case. Use a writing frame to help structure the argument if needed.	Share and evaluate work in progress. Encourage constructive feedback. Praise convincing points of argument.	
Friday	Discuss the ambiguities in Silver's character and relate to life experience. Are real people wholly good or bad? Discuss other familiar characters in fiction: are they presented as wholly good or bad?	Character comparisons (as above).	Character comparisons (as above). Refine and improve argument, taking account of feedback.	Ask for volunteers to present the argument for and against. Discuss which argument is most convincing. Have a secret ballot to answer the debate question.	

WEEK 2	Shared text work	Group	Independent	Plenary
Monday	General discussion about film openings. View the opening sequence of a film (not *Treasure Island*) and use as a stimulus for discussing the language of film. Revisit the opening passage of *Treasure Island*. Who is telling the story?	Select a challenge from the poster.	Paired work: consider how you would film the opening of *Treasure Island*. Storyboard ideas, making notes about camera angles, music, sound effects, etc. (see p. 77). Pairs to fours: compare and evaluate the storyboards, noting similarities and differences.	Whole class: feedback focusing on what the pairs like about each other's work.
Tuesday	View an opening sequence of a *Treasure Island* film. Discuss first responses. Did they like/dislike the opening? What mood was created? What happens to the narrator in the film version? Start to make a list of similarities and differences with the novel.	Select a challenge from the poster.	Watch the opening again. In pairs or small groups, discuss and note the similarities and differences with the novel. Provide a list of prompts to aid discussion, e.g. character, setting, order of the story, narrator, mood, dialogue.	Make a chart showing the similarities and differences and consider the reasons why some changes may have been made. Consider the influence of genre on the way character is portrayed.

WEEK 2	Shared text work	Group	Independent	Plenary
Wednesday	View representations of Silver's character in at least two film versions. Review the previous week's work on Silver's character. Introduce the idea of concept designs for film. Concept artwork is often available on the microsites devoted to specific films (e.g. *Pirates of the Caribbean*).	Select a challenge from the poster.	Create an annotated concept design for a film adaptation of Long John Silver. Ask the children to suggest an actor that they would like to play the role and to explain their choice.	Share the work in progress. Ask the children to explain how closely related the designs are to Stevenson's text. Where they have intentionally made changes, ask for explanations.
Thursday	Reread sheet 6.2. View one adaptation of the scene. Are there any surprises? What similarities and differences?	Select a challenge from the poster.	In small groups, view a different adaptation of the same scene. Note changes and discuss the effectiveness of the interpretation. This works well if two contrasting adaptations are used, e.g. Charlton Heston version, *Treasure Planet*.	Feedback from the group studying the second film extract. Discuss differences and similarities of different versions.
Friday	Review work in progress. Consider how changes in Silver's mood and circumstances might be reflected in changes to the costume design (e.g. At the Sign of the Spyglass, Ship's Cook, Captain of the Mutineers).	Select a challenge from the poster.	Continue to develop concept designs for other characters.	Summarise: What have we learnt about adapting a book for the cinema. Consider restraints and possibilities.

WEEK 3	Shared text work	Group	Independent	Plenary
Monday	Features of a good opening. Create list of criteria from the children's suggestions. Read and annotate the opening of the novel (Photocopiable sheet 4.3).	Compare and evaluate openings from *Silver's Revenge* and/or *The Curse of Treasure Island* (Photocopiable sheet 4.4 and 4.5).	Write the beginning of an adventure story using some of the features discussed.	Share work in progress and evaluate each other's work using criteria created in shared text work.
Tuesday	Chapter endings – cliffhangers. Read, discuss and annotate the extract 'Inside the apple barrel' (Photocopiable sheet 4.2).	Compare and evaluate openings from *Silver's Revenge* and/or *The Curse of Treasure Island*.	Create freeze frames of the moment that Jim overhears mutineers' plans. Bring each frame to life and ask the children to improvise the scene for 30 seconds then refreeze.	Share one or two improvisations. Model writing dialogue using conventions for presenting direct speech. Draw on the improvisations to consider different ways in which plot might develop.

WEEK 3	Shared text work	Group	Independent	Plenary
Wednesday	Review knowledge of narrative structure. Introduce Photocopiable sheet 4.1 and clarify terminology.	Compare and evaluate openings from *Silver's Revenge* and/or *The Curse of Treasure Island*.	In groups, identify key moments in the story and complete sheet 4.1.	Share completed planning sheets and consider the selection of different moments. Ask groups to justify their choices. Negotiate a final selection of key moments.
Thursday	Review completed sheet 4.1 from the previous lesson. Reread the opening Chapter and construct a freeze frame to represent the story opening. Ask children for suggestions to extend and improve.	Compare and evaluate openings from *Silver's Revenge* and/or *The Curse of Treasure Island* (see p. 43).	Allocate key moments to different groups. Referring to text, ask groups to create a freeze frame for their allocated moment.	Share and discuss freeze frames. Use thought tracking to explore characters' thoughts. Ask for words that suggest the mood conveyed in each image and list on the board. Extend vocabulary by looking for similar words in a thesaurus. Chart the changing moods throughout the story.
Friday	Reconstruct the freeze frame for opening of the story from the previous lesson. Reread passage and identify two key quotations that sum up the opening. Select one, giving reasons for choice.	Groups refine freeze frames taking account of feedback from the previous lesson. Referring to the relevant passage select key quotations for their freeze frames.	Groups select key quotations for their freeze frames. Write the quotations on large sheets of paper.	Arrange the freeze frames and quotations to construct a tableaux of *Treasure Island*. Allow time to 'rehearse' the tableaux. Evaluate: take suggestions for improvement. Perform tableaux for an audience.

11   Reading other books by Stevenson

Dr Jekyll and Mr Hyde: 'The mad scientist'

Dr Jekyll and Mr Hyde (1886) tells the story of society doctor, Dr Jekyll, who invents a potion in order to test his theory that man has a dual nature. He drinks the formula and under its influence becomes Edward Hyde, an amoral creature who acts on animal instinct and commits hideous crimes. Gradually, Jekyll becomes addicted to the transformation into Hyde. The novel is set in Victorian London, a city that was both rich and beautiful but which bred terrible poverty and squalor behind its beautiful façade. The setting reflects the novel's major theme: that appearances are deceptive.

The nineteenth century was a period of scientific discovery and invention. Jekyll starts his work with good intention but his vanity leads him to more extreme experiments which eventually spiral out of control. Dr Jekyll belongs to a long tradition of 'the mad scientist' in English literature which dates back to at least Christopher Marlowe's *Faustus*. In western literature, the mad scientist is often portrayed as a character who creates trouble. Other mad scientists in 'classic' literature include Dr Frankenstein in Mary Shelley's *Frankenstein*, Dr Griffin in H. G. Wells' *The Invisible Man* and Captain Nemo in Jules Verne's *20,000 Leagues Under the Sea*. Mad scientists are also a feature in films, such as the recent film adaptation of Marvel comic's The Incredible Hulk: *Hulk* (2003). Bruce Banner is a respectable scientist who by means of chemical substances transforms into the evil side of his personality. In common with other monster/scientist stories the evil creation eventually kills the creator. The Hulk is a direct descendant of Stevenson's story.

Humorous examples of 'mad scientists' are common in children's films and programmes, such as Cartoon Network's *Dexter's Laboratory* and Disney's *Honey I Shrunk the Kids*.

Activities

Read one of the adaptations of Stevenson's *Dr Jekyll and Mr Hyde*, such as Chris Mould's graphic version or John Grant's retelling for Usborne Classic series. After reading the story, investigate the role of the mad scientist in literature.

- Focus on Dr Jekyll to identify some characteristics of the mad scientist.
- What other stories, including film and comic versions, that feature 'mad scientists' are familiar to the children?
- Ask the children to draw on their knowledge in order to make a collection of stories and images that feature mad scientists. Introduce them to some early examples (e.g. Frankenstein, Professor Moriarty, Dr Griffin etc).

- What similarities and differences do they notice in the ways in which the scientists are represented?
- In small groups or pairs, ask the children to categorise the scientists by genre (e.g. horror, comedy, fantasy). Do any patterns emerge in the way in which the 'mad scientist' functions in the stories? How does the effect differ in horror and comedy?
- Has the image of the mad scientist changed over time? Look at some examples from the nineteenth century and compare them with some modern examples. What are the similarities? What are the differences?
- Write a short story featuring a mad scientist.
- Select and read some passages that build up the character of the mad scientist in a range of stories. After reading and annotating the passages, ask the children to paint or draw the characters, referring to the text.
- Compare the story of Dr Jekyll and Mr Hyde with the 2003 film *Hulk*. In what ways are the stories similar and different?

Kidnapped: The Scottish Novel

Stevenson's *Kidnapped* (1886) is an adventure story and historical novel set during the Jacobite rebellion in Scotland. First published in installments in the boy's adventure magazine *Young Folks*, it recounts the thrilling adventures of David Balfour, a 16-year-old orphan who must learn to make his way in the world before he can claim his inheritance, and Alan Breck, a Jacobite and supporter of James II. In spite of their different political persuasions, Alan befriends David and remains loyal to him.

Throughout the Middle Ages the relationship between Scotland and England was tense and hostilities often erupted. After the death of Queen Elizabeth 1 in 1603, the throne passed to King James who became James I of England and VI of Scotland. Despite this, the process of unification of the two crowns was not straightforward. In 1685, after the death of Charles II, his brother James became king. However, James was not a popular monarch and in 1688 fled to France with his son (James) and grandson (Charles Edward). The Stuarts lived in exile. In 1707, the Act of Union led to the dissolution of the Scottish parliament, and in 1714 the throne passed to George I from the House of Hanover. In 1715 the Jacobites made their first attempt to restore the Stuarts to the throne, but Prince James was not the figure-head they had hoped for and the campaign lost heart. A further attempt was made in 1745 by Prince Charles Edward: 'Bonnie Prince Charlie'. Although this time the pretender was able to march into Edinburgh, ultimately, without the support of the English, the uprising failed again. Bonnie Prince Charlie fled into exile and the Jacobites were hunted and persecuted.

Kidnapped is set during this period of turmoil, during the reign of George II. David Balfour is proud to be the subject of George II. At one point in the story, when Colin Campbell inquires about his relationship with James of Glen, David says, 'I am neither of his people nor yours, but an honest subject of King George, owing no man and fearing no man.' Although he is ostensibly a royalist at heart, David is attracted to the romantic, charismatic Jacobites. Alan Breck is a Jacobite.

Stevenson wrote a sequel to *Kidnapped* called *Catriona*. It was published in 1893. *Kidnapped* can be used as a stimulating introduction to this period of Scottish history. Read some extracts from the novel or one of the abridged versions. After reading you might engage in some of the following activities.

Activities

- Compare Stevenson's portrayal of David Balfour and Alan Breck. Where do Stevenson's sympathies appear to lie?
- Compare the lowland and highland settings in the novels. The novel begins in the lowlands, moves to the highlands and ultimately returns to David's home in the lowlands.
- *Kidnapped* is a serious book which is full of action. The introduction of eccentric characters lightens the mood. Look closely at an example (e.g. Mr. Rankeillor's feigned forgetfulness). Ask the children to think of other stories they have read where humorous characters lighten an otherwise dark or serious story.
- *Kidnapped* is an adventure story. Rewrite part of the story in a different genre (e.g. as a soap opera, a news feature, a documentary).
- Use rainbow groups to research the history of the period. Each rainbow group investigates a different aspect of the period using a range of resources, including books and the internet (e.g. Bonnie Prince Charlie's flight to Skye, Culloden, etc.). When the research is complete re-form the home groups. The children report back what they have found out to their home group and the group composes a non-chronological report.

12   Poster challenges

Challenge 1 Pirate Parley

This challenge is an investigation into language origins and meanings. It is designed to develop children's knowledge of reference sources including dictionaries of phrase and fable, dictionaries of word origins (etymology) and internet resources. They will need to use some resources that are not specifically written for children as well as those that are. Children should be encouraged to check for meanings and origins in more than one source comparing information. Words and phrases can be laminated, cut out and distributed to small groups.

After completing the challenge, the children could be invited to create a display for the school library. Pirate words and phrases can be displayed in large speech bubbles alongside the collection of reference materials along with questions devised by the children for others to investigate. Children may also want to browse through the reference materials as well as carrying out the focused challenge.

Resources

John Ayto (2002) *Oxford School Dictionary of Word Origins*, Oxford University Press
Glynis Chantrell (ed.) (2002) *The Oxford Dictionary of Word Histories*, Oxford University Press
Olivia Isil (1996) *When a Loose Cannon Flogs a Dead Horse There's the Devil to Pay: Seafaring Words in Everyday Speech*
Richard McClosky (2002) *Salty Dog Talk: The Nautical Origins of Everyday Expressions*
Adrian Room (ed.) (2000) *Brewer's Dictionary of Phrase and Fable*
Adam Room (1999) *Brewer's Dictionary of Names: People, Places and Things*
A Pirate's glossary http://homepage.mac.com/crabola/PirateGlossary/Menu22.html
Talk Like a Pirate http://talklikeapirateday.com/index.php?page=PirateWords
A Pirate's Vocabulary http://www.puzzlepirates.com/docs/vocabulary.html

Challenge 2 Pirates: Fact and Fiction

This activity is designed to provide an opportunity for children to find out about pirates from a wide range of sources and to compare the fictional representation in *Treasure Island* and other pirate stories and films they have read and seen (see resource list p. 91). The children should also be encouraged to think about bias and opinion in the factual material.

Challenge 3 Comic Strip

Before carrying out this activity the children should have had opportunities for browsing a range of comics and graphic novels which use a variety of styles (e.g. *Manga, Beano, The Simpsons, Rupert* etc.) and have discussed in groups some of the conventions used to tell a story in this way. They might have looked at Chris Mould's graphic version of *Treasure Island* and *Dr Jekyll and Mr Hyde*. The task is to retell a favourite scene from *Treasure Island* in comic book form. A variation is to allocate different key scenes to the children to produce a graphic version for the class or school library. This transformation task requires the children to think about narrative structure, telling a story in words and pictures, building suspense and audience.

Resource

Scott McCloud (1994) *Understanding Comics*, HarperCollins.

Challenge 4 Design a Book Jacket

This task invites children to design a book jacket for a favourite Stevenson book. They might have a look at a range of book jackets before completing this task.

Select bibliography of Stevenson's works

Novels

Treasure Island (1883)
Kidnapped (1886)
The Strange Case of Dr Jekyll and Mr Hyde (1886)
The Black Arrow (1888)
The Master of Ballentrae (1889)
Catriona (1893)
The Weir of Hermiston (1896) (posthumously)

Poetry

A Child's Garden of Verses (1885)

Other writings

An Inland Voyage (1878)
Edinburgh: Picturesque Notes (1878)
Travels with a Donkey in the Cevennes (1879)
The Silverado Squatters (1884)
In the South Seas (1896) (posthumously)
Letters of Robert Louis Stevenson to his Family and Friends (1899) (posthumously)
The Art of Writing and Other Essays (1905) (posthumously)

Stevenson's non-fiction writing provides a wealth of autobiographical material. There are several in-print versions of these texts, but much of the material can be downloaded from the internet. See the resource list on p. 91, or type the selected title into a search engine, such as Google, to bring up sites where these materials can be viewed and printed.

Resource list and bibliography

Resource list: Robert Louis Stevenson
Teachers' resources

Bell, Ian (1992), *Dreams of Exile: Robert Louis Stevenson – a Biography*, Mainstream Publishing
Callow, Philip (2001), *Louis: the life of Robert Louis Stevenson*, Constable and Robinson
Carpenter, A.S. (1997), *Robert Louis Stevenson: finding Treasure Island*, Lerner Publications
Chesterton, G.K. (2001), *Robert Louis Stevenson*, House of Stratus
Davies, Hunter (1994), *The Teller of Tales: In Search of Robert Louis Stevenson*, Sinclair Stevenson
McLynn, Frank (1994), *Robert Louis Stevenson: A Biography*, Pimlico
Mehew, Ernest (ed.) (2001), *Selected Letters of Robert Louis Stevenson*, Yale University Press
Nolan, Scott Allen (1994), *Robert Louis Stevenson: Life, Literature and the Silver Screen*, Macfarland and Company
Rankin, Nicholas (2001), *Dead Man's Chest: Travels after Robert Louis Stevenson*, Wiedenfeld & Nicholson
Sawyers, June Skinner (ed.) (2002), *Dreams of Elsewhere: Selected Travel Writing*, The In Pinn
Styles, M. (1998), *From the Garden to the Street: Three Hundred Years of Poetry for Children*, Cassell (Chapter 8)

Pupils' resources

Gamble, N. (2003), *Favourite Classic Writers*, Hodder Wayland

Selected websites

The Robert Louis Stevenson website
    wwwesterni.unibg.it/siti_esterni/rls/rls.htm
Edinburgh Picturesque notes
    www.worldwideschool.org/library/books/geo/travel/EdinburghPicturesqueNotes/toc.html
Biographical information
    www.sc.edu/library/spcoll/britlit/rls/rls.html
Robert Louis Stevenson on stamps and banknotes
    www.trussel.com/rls/rls.htm
Images of Robert Louis Stevenson
    www.esterni.unibg.it/siti_esterni/rls/images.htm

Online selected writings of Robert Louis Stevenson, including essays on writing
www.blackmask.com/page.php?do=page&cat_id=114

Stevenson's letters
www.worldwideschool.org/library/books/lit/literarystudies/TheLettersofRobertLouisStevenson

New York Times: Stevenson's obituary
www.nytimes.com/learning/general/onthisday/bday/113.html

Extended review of Graham Balfour's biography *The Life of Robert Louis Stevenson*
www.theatlantic.com/unbound/classrev/rlsteve.htm

Entry from *Discovering Scottish Writers*
www.slainte.org.uk/scotauth/stevedsw.htm

Information about Samoa
www.jpacific.com/samoa/samoa1.html

The Stevenson House website, includes images of the interior of Heriot Row
www.stevenson-house.co.uk/terms.htm

Video

Famous Authors: Robert Louis Stevenson, Academy Videos

Resource list: *Treasure Island*

Treasure Island editions

Robert Louis Stevenson (1994), *Treasure Island* (Puffin Classics), Puffin

Robert Louis Stevenson, Michael Morpurgo (foreword) (2001), *Treasure Island*, Kingfisher

Robert Louis Stevenson, Justin Todd (illustrator), *Treasure Island*, Chrysalis Books

Robert Louis Stevenson, Colin McNaughton (illustrator), *Treasure Island*, Macmillan

Graphic version

Chris Mould (2001), *Treasure Island*, Oxford University Press

Related books including sequels

J. M. Barrie (1994) *Peter Pan*, Puffin Classic

Francis Bryan (2002), *Jim Hawkins and The Curse of Treasure Island*, Orion

Robert Leeson (1978), *Silver's Revenge*, Collins

J. Meade Faulkener (1994), *Moonfleet*, Puffin Classics

Treasure Planet Novelisation, Disney Press

Robinsonnades: old and new

J. D. Wyss, William H. G. Kingston (trans.) (1996), *Swiss Family Robinson*, Puffin

R. M. Ballantyne (1982), *The Coral Island*, Puffin

Scott O' Dell (1966), *Island of the Blue Dolphins*, Puffin

Theodore Taylor (1969), *The Cay*, Puffin

Michael Morpurgo (2000), *Kensuke's Kingdom*, Mammoth

Audio
Robert Louis Stevenson, Alan Cumming (narrator) (1997), *Treasure Island*, Puffin Audio
Robert Louis Stevenson, Windsor Davies (narrator) (2003), *Treasure Island*, Ladybird Books
Robert Louis Stevenson, David Buck (narrator), *Treasure Island*, Cover-to-cover, BBC
J. Meade Faulkener (1999), *Moonfleet*, Puffin Classics

Films
(1950) *Treasure Island*, Disney (U certificate)
(1990) *Treasure Island*, Warner (PG certificate)
(1996) *Muppet Treasure Island*, Disney (U certificate)
(2000) *Treasure Island*, (12 certificate)
(2002) *Treasure Planet*, Disney (U certificate)
The 1990 Warner film starring Charlton Heston as Long John Silver with Oliver Reed as Billy Bones, Christopher Lee as Blind Pew and Julian Glover as Dr Livesey is closest to the spirit of Stevenson's text and includes much of the original dialogue. The sailing sequences also provide good detail of what was involved in sailing a ship. *Treasure Island* (1997), BBC (PG certificate).

Websites
Treasure Island: www.ukoln.ac.uk/services/treasure/
Treasure Planet: http://disney.go.com/disneyvideos/animatedfilms/treasureplanet/main.html

Pirates: books for teachers
David Cordingly (1997), *Under the Black Flag*, Thomson Education. A revisionist history of the golden age of piracy which draws on original archive material and records to provide a realistic study of pirates and their lives that refutes many of the colourful myths about the era.
Angus Konstam (1998), *Pirates 1660–1730*, Osprey

Pirates: books for children (fiction and fictionalised fact)
Tony Bradman (2003), *The Kingfisher Treasury of Pirate Stories*, Kingfisher
Patrick Burston (2003), *Pirates of Doom*, Walker Books
Colin Hawkins (2001), *Pirate's Log*, Picture Lions
Richard Platt, Chris Riddell (illus.) (2001), *Pirate Diary: The Journal of Jake Carpenter*, Walker Books
Richard Walker (2001), *My Very First Book of Pirates*, Barefoot Books
Peter Carter and Korky Paul (illus.) (1991), *Captain Teachum's Buried Treasure*, OUP
Sally Byford (2000), *Captain Pugwash*, Red Fox
Jeff Nicholson (2002), *Colonia*, AIT–Planet Lar (Graphic novel series)
Jeremy Strong (1997) *The Indoor Pirates*, Puffin
Jeremy Strong (1998) *The Indoor Pirates on Treasure Island*, Puffin
Simon Furman (2003) *Transformers: Space Pirates*, Titan
Richard Hamilton (2003) *Violet and the Mean and Rotten Pirates*, Bloomsbury
Susannah Leigh (2003) *Uncle Pete's Pirate Adventures*, Usborne

Pirates: books for children (information)
John Farman (2000), *The Short and Bloody History of Pirates,* Red Fox
Richard Platt (2002), *Discovering Pirates,* Haldane Mason
Richard Platt, Tina Chambers (2000), *Pirate* (Eyewitness Books) Dorling Kindersley
Chris Powling and Chris Mould (illus.) (2003), *Pirates,* Oxford University Press.
Philip Steele (2003), *Pirates: Discovery Series,* Lorenz Books
Philip Steele (2001), *Pirates and Pioneers,* Kingfisher

Websites
Pirate images website:
    www.piratehaven.org/~beej/pirates/
Pirates fact and legend:
    www.piratesinfo.com/main.php
Pirates Providence:
    www.inkyfingers.com/pyrates/index.html
Edward Teach:
    tinpan.fortunecity.com/lennon/897/teach.html
Pirates of the Caribbean:
    http://pirates.movies.go.com/

Ships and maritime history: books, websites and video
Angus Konstam and Tony Bryan (illus.) (2003), *Pirate Ship 1660 –1730,* Osprey
National Maritime Museum:
    www.nmm.ac.uk
The Mariners Museum:
    www.mariner.org/(2000)
    Age of Sail: Galleons and Pirate Ships, DD Video

For Product Safety Concerns and Information please contact our EU
representative GPSR@taylorandfrancis.com
Taylor & Francis Verlag GmbH, Kaufingerstraße 24, 80331 München, Germany

www.ingramcontent.com/pod-product-compliance
Lightning Source LLC
Chambersburg PA
CBHW081847230426
43669CB00018B/2851